SHUFTO

Tom,

Thank you for the support!!

God bless,

Dwigh James

SHUFTO

MY UNIQUE JOURNEY FROM SUDAN, EGYPT, TO THE U.S.A

OLWAK "SHUFTO" JENARO

NEW DEGREE PRESS

SHUFTO

My Unique Journey from Sudan, Egypt to the U.S.A

ISBN   978-1-63676-835-9 *Paperback*

978-1-63730-207-1 *Kindle Ebook*

978-1-63730-279-8 *Ebook*

To my mother, I dedicate this book to you because there is no one on this planet who could've put up with me the way you have all of my life. For that, you deserve all my thanks and gratitude. You raised me to be honest and true to myself no matter the circumstance and have always been supportive. You've sacrificed so much for our family over the years, and you have not allowed those sacrifices to change who you are. Thank you for remaining true to yourself and to all of us, and thank you for always being the sweet, loving, caring, gentle soul you are.

Contents

Acknowledgments

To all seven of my siblings, thank you for helping me learn how to be a big brother. Life hasn't been easy on any of us growing up but know you've inspired me to be a better person. As the oldest, know I have often thought about how my actions may serve as a good or bad example for all of you. To Aken and Moum in particular, please know I have tried to do my best as your big brother in Sudan, in Egypt, as well as here in the US.

To the rest of my family and friends, I believe it is by design each and every one of you came into my life at the exact moment you were meant to be there. It was not by accident each and every one of you influenced my life the way you all have. Thank you to all my family:

Abas Omar, Abuna, Fr. Ronald Sajdak, Amer Lam, Anders Gunnersen, André Sadoff, Ann Marie Szpakowska, Ann Marie Szpakowska, Anthony Christiano, Benane Awejok Akurkuch, Benjamin Macaluso, Charity Niphong, Cynthia Schilling, Emmanuel Obunadike, Eric Koester, George Theodor, Greg Bennett, James Budu, Jean D'amour Boyi, Jebeh Sambola, Jessica Smith, Jordan Kawaya, Kevin Mckenzie, Leyla Fagory, Liana Wingenbach, Mahawa Osei, Mary

Tilahunm, Mimi Abdalla, Minh Le, Nancy Nsengiyumva, Nate Buckley, Niveen Laa, Nyibol Deng, Okach Ojway, Oscar Brown, Oter Amon, Paige Buxbaum, Rahim Melon, Rehan Cyer, Roberto Cruz, ROTA Development Group Inc., Rout Niel, Sasha Waskosky, Sebet Thon

Introduction

PREFACE

I decided to write this book to share my story with the world, a story filled with struggle, hardships, and so many twists and turns I lost count. It is also a story full of hope, blessings, sheer luck, and life-changing moments. For good or bad, "*Shufta*," meaning "I've seen," and experienced so many things over the first thirteen years of my life. It took a long time to understand and learn how to process most of it. When I finally did, I was a refugee kid living halfway across the world in a completely foreign land. I had no idea whether I would ever have the chance to lay eyes on my birthplace again.

CHAPTER 1

Reasons Why

We often hear about the horrors in refugee camps and the terrible wars driving people out of their homes. We see pictures and videos of displaced people in refugee camps on foreign soil, living in unbelievable conditions no human being should ever have to endure. In the 1990s, most of those photos depicted children and women living in overcrowded camps, such as Kakuma in Northwestern Kenya. Mothers, children, and the elderly often lived together in small makeshift tents with no running water or indoor plumbing. Orphans who had lost parents, siblings, and other relatives in Sudan's civil war were often pictured in the littered streets of Kakuma and in other refugee camps such as Pugnido Refugee Camp in Ethiopia.[1]

Those were often the images that came to mind for most people wherever they thought about refugees in the 1990s. Unfortunately, very little has changed over the years, and the number of refugees and displaced people remains high. In fact, there are now more refugees and displaced people around the world then there were over two decades ago. This

---

1   *"Africa's biggest refugee camps,"* Africa Facts, Accessed March 5, 2021.

is a direct result of the number of increased conflicts globally, particularly in the Middle East, the north, and parts of Sub-Saharan Africa, as well as Southeast Asia. What we don't often see is photos of displaced people who do not necessarily look like the typical "refugee." Although it is absolutely imperative to continue bring attention to the most affected refugee populations, it is also important to shed light on the different conditions and experiences all refugees face worldwide.

To shine the necessary spotlight on the many conflicts around the world continuing to produce more and more refugees, we all have a responsibility to speak up. People and governments around the world can influence and help prevent many of the conflicts producing refugees. Yes, it is no easy task, but if we all did our part, it is possible to limit and reduce the number of people (often civilians) affected by senseless violence throughout many parts of the world. The reality is—the people often suffering the most and experiencing the worst horrors of war—are always civilians. Women, children, and the elderly.

Telling my story is one action helping shine light on one part of the refugee experience. My experience is quite different from the war ravaged one regularly seen on the news. This other refugee experience also has devastating effects on many families, individuals, and their communities. People felt they had no other option but to leave their homes, families, and everything else behind in hopes of a better life elsewhere. Their stories are worth sharing, and that is the refugee journey my family and I experienced.

Another reason I felt compelled to write this book was for myself. I've struggled from time to time with trying to understand and make sense of parts of my life. A deep reflection into my childhood and into my past experiences seemed to be the best course of action to help me process and work through those challenges. As I revisited parts of my past and recalled childhood memories, I began to realize some of those childhood experiences may have been traumatic in nature but were never acknowledged or properly addressed. This was the main reason I titled the book *SHUFTO*.

Shufto is an Arabic word which means "seen it." This word is the best representation for my story, not only because it is befitting of my personal journey, but because it also happens to be my name. *Yes,* I said my name. It is in fact a very unusual name, probably in every language known to man. Nonetheless, it is a name given to me from birth by my creative mother. Imagine growing up with such a name in an environment that does not consider bullying to be a serious problem. Imagine having to live with, and constantly deal with, the reality everyone thinks your name is some kind of joke. Imagine always being asked to explain the meaning behind it at the age of five or six, as if you were in consultation with your parents and had a vote on the decision. Imagine trying to understand at such a young age what could have possibly pushed your mother to think that was a good decision. Imagine constantly wondering, *Why? Why me?*

As terrible as it was growing up with the name *Shufto*, it wasn't my legal name. On paper and to the world outside of my neighborhood, my official name is *Olwak*. It is my given *Cøllø* name. *Cøllø.* also known as *Shilluk*, is my native language, and the name *Olwak* has prominence in my family. The name is derived from the *Cøllø* word "*lwak*," which can be described as a large open barn where cattle are kept. In *Cøllø* culture, similar to most South Sudanese cultures, it is common practice to name children after grandparents and elders in the family.

I was named after my grandfather's elder brother, a beloved and well-respected member of our community. Being named after Grandpa *Olwak* is meaningful and an honor. It always made me feel a sense of connection to him in spirit and gave me a sense of responsibility as well, a sense of responsibility to live up to his legacy, and to always be a unifying figure and proctor to my family similar to a *lwak*. Subconsciously, I think I've always relied on the strong meaning behind my name and often used it as a source to guide me in the right direction in life.

When I reflect on different stages in my life, I realized there were often very special people by my side. Individuals and groups have played pivotal roles guiding and helping to take care of me throughout the years. Chief amongst them is my mother, grandparents, other family members especially when I was a child. Later on, I had close friends and mentors who have changed my life for the better, and I consider all of them to be heaven-sent. Without them, there is no telling how my life would have turn out. As a result of their collective influences in my life, I owe each and every one of them a great deal for their guidance and personal investment in me.

I attribute a huge part of the reason I'm passionate about my work in the community, especially with young people, to be a result of that personal experience. To start your life in a difficult poverty-stricken environment and survive through years of struggle and uncertainty can test anyone's faith. It can also seem hopeless. But to find yourself one day presented with an opportunity to make the best of what life has to offer, and to be surrounded my people wishing nothing but the best for you is powerful and life-changing to say the least.

In this life, each and every one of us has a purpose or a calling. You may not discover that purpose early on in life, and it may take years or decades to figure it out as it does for some people. The journey to discover this calling can take many paths for different people. However, not everyone is fortunate enough to choose their own path. Throughout most of the world, the opportunity to pursue dreams and goals is a privilege afforded to few. Nonetheless, this does not mean it is impossible for others to find ways to overcome those challenges and limitations.

There are people born with an innate ability to pinpoint their life's purpose. They have absolute clarity and little doubt about what they believe is their purpose for being on this planet. Those individuals are often passionate about their professions and regard them as more than a simple job; it's a calling. Doctors and nurses, for example, are at the top of that list; their purpose in society is to save lives. One cannot be an effective doctor, nurse, or any other healthcare professional if they do not believe in the importance of their work.

Teachers and educators are also amongst those groups of people. It takes a special kind of person to choose this career path. The best educators are the most effective because of their character and desire to help mold, influence, and shape the minds of their students. There are other attractive professions for such individuals with a clear view of their calling and purpose, such as in the sciences, religion, and public service.

Growing up in Khartoum, Sudan, I always believed my calling was clear. I thought my purpose in life was to follow in my father's footsteps and study medicine to become a doctor. At the time, my father was pursuing his education as a medical student. I have to admit at the age of five or six,

I was not well acclimated with the true meaning of "life's purpose." I did not quite understand nor care much about the process of achieving that goal. Like any child, I thought, *If dad was doing it, so can I. That would surely make both of us happy.* Well, it turned out life isn't that simple, and it took a long time and a series of life-changing experiences to learn that important lesson.

CHAPTER 2

First Memory

———

One of my first memories is from early childhood as a toddler. I don't know how I'm still able to vividly recall this, but it is a dream-like memory that seems to be stamped into my memory bank. At the time, I couldn't have been older than a year or two, but for some reason I'm able to recall the events particularly well. It all happened one calm summer evening in a town called Geigar.

I was born in Khartoum, the capital of modern day (North) Sudan in March of 1989. At the time, my grandparents lived in Geigar, a small town just north of Renk, Upper Nile State, in present-day South Sudan. My mother took me to visit my maternal grandparents for the first time so they could see their grandson and her firstborn. The journey from Khartoum to Geigar was a lengthy one and normally lasted a full day, often on an old vessel slowly working its way up the White Nile.

I can still remember details from a few of the other trips my mom and I later took to Geigar when I was a few years older. For instance, the calm, cool, and bright mornings we spent together drinking hot tea before reaching our destination. There were the smells and sounds of the water passing by from the river as we inched closer to the town. The sight of greenery and vegetation along the Nile banks never failed to indicate we were no longer in the hot deserts of Northern Sudan. It was always amazing to see Southern Sudan in those early morning hours and to see and hear birds chirping so loudly. During those mornings, the gentle breeze smelled and felt different, and my level of excitement always piqued because I knew in a few short hours we would finally be standing in my grandparents' courtyard.

Out of all the visits to see my grandparents, the most interesting was the first one with my mother. The very first memory I have of it was of me sitting on the ground outside of a *Cøllø* (*Shilluk*) hut build out of mud with a roof made of straws. It was a warm, cloudy, but calm evening, typical during the rainy months between April or May through October. During that moment, I suddenly noticed the ground around turning dark, darker than the soil I was playing on just minutes before with my mom. The exact details and image of the house have blurred over the years, but what occurred next is the single reason this memory remains unforgettable.

My mother, my grandfather, and my grandmother, as well as a few other adults were outside in the courtyard with me. It's difficult to recall all the faces, but I remember feeling their presence. There were other people inside the hut just yards away from where we were siting. At one point all the adults around me jumped up from their seats and ran toward the hut in a dramatic fashion. It happened so suddenly, as if there was an emergency. Everyone, including my mother, was gone in an instant and I was suddenly all alone. No one, not a single soul, was in sight. There wasn't a dog, a goat, or even a single chicken running around, which was strange because my grandmother always kept some farm animal around.

As I sat there on the ground watching everyone including my mom run off to figure out what was going on, I noticed a large, unusual presence all around me. At first, I couldn't figure out what this strange figure was, and I did not have any idea where it came from. All I knew was I could no longer see anyone or anything past this figure in front of my eyes blocking my view. I could no longer see the hut, and all I could hear were faint panicking voices off in the distance.

I was surrounded by a massive snake. It's unclear whether it was a python, a boa, or a different subspecies of large snakes. I recall this massive reptile circled around me for some time, but I did not see its head or eyes, and I did not hear it hissing or making any other sounds. Time seemed to freeze, but after a while its presence seemed to slowly fade away, and before I noticed the figure completely vanished into thin air. The entire time, I did not move a muscle. I didn't cry; I didn't feel frightened; and in fact I think I was fascinated by this strange creature and had no idea I may have been in danger. I knew nothing of what was happening, and I knew nothing of what could happen next, and I certainly did not know my life could have ended at that very moment.

I cannot explain what was going through my mind. Perhaps I was curious about what I was seeing through my baby eyes, truly ignorant of the world around me and its dangers. Or it's possible I had no clear concept of life or death, and therefore had no reason to be afraid. It's also possible because I was alone with this creature, with no one else around and nothing disturbed or provoked it to react one way or another. Maybe I simply wasn't the livestock it was seeking for dinner. I don't know. What I do know is I am still alive and here now.

It's strange my recollection of this "memory" still feels and seems so clear in my mind. I was so young, and yet I haven't forgotten it. In all honesty, it is difficult to say for certain whether those series of events actually occurred the way I recall, or whether it was all a product of my imagination. It is possible those events were simply a part of some strange dream that somehow weaved itself into my memory bank, disguised as true memories or not. It's also important to mention during that time in Geigar, I suffered a severe illness while in the care of my grandparents. My mother had returned to Khartoum for a short while days after we arrived, and I stayed behind with my grandparents. I'm sure I was happy to be there with Grandpa and Grandma, whom I adored, but my time with them in Geigar the first time around was short-lived according to Mom.

It is entirely possible and likely the severe illness I suffered may have been a near-death experience that manifested into this strange dream or memory. My mother later told me she was so afraid of losing me she rushed back to Geigar and brought me back to Khartoum for treatment. Every time I visited after that first experience, I seemed to always fall ill, which may have perpetuated this dream or memory of my close brush with death. The manifestation of the large snake may have been an attempt by my young mind to make sense of my dire situation, an attempt to understand the reality of this frightening life or death experience, forever burned into my existence.

Regardless of the true nature of this experience, I have a constant reminder I'm here in this world for a reason. I am reminded to be grateful and never take anything for granted. It goes without saying life can be unpredictable. For many people, everyday can be a challenge, and sometimes it is easy to lose sight of what's important. We can easily get caught up in the cycle and routine of everyday life and never take the time to appreciate what matters to us most. Life, family, health, and wellness are important factors to keep in mind, and faith in the possibilities life has to offer should be at the top all of our lists.

I understand life is not always simple, and I understand things are not always as clear as we wish them to be. Yes, sometimes things happen in life we may not understand and cannot explain in simple terms, or at all. This does not mean we should ignore them and pretend they never happened. We should still try. We may not know the value of a major event or events at the moment it happens, but that does not mean it is meaningless. Overtime, we may begin to realize and understand the invaluable lessons embedded in those events. Be patient. Life may not provide a clear roadmap to follow your dreams and accomplish all the goals you set forth. This does not mean you should abandon them and give up on yourself, or the people you care about most. Have faith. Have faith in yourself, and have faith in God. He will see you through it all. Lastly, you may face a task that seems impossible to complete and can be overwhelming. This does not mean you should quit and give up. Find a way. Nothing is impossible to accomplish if you are willing to work hard and give it your all.

This experience was the very first meaningful experience I can remember, and it is also the one that taught me the most important value—the value of life. Yes, life is often difficult and unpredictable among other things, but it is also full of wonders that make it worth every moment. My story is one iteration, and I am grateful to share it in hopes of reminding the world it is a blessing to be alive and to have survived countless trials and tribulations. To still be here, healthy and well, and to have the opportunity to share my journey with the world is a once-in-a-lifetime opportunity not everyone receives. Be grateful.

CHAPTER 3

Shigla Haj Yousif

In Khartoum, the capital of Sudan, we lived in a neighborhood called *Shigla Haj Yousif.* I grew up in a traditional household surrounded by family. My mother and I lived with my aunts, uncles, and my grandparents. Our home was built in typical Sudanese style on a three-hundred to four-hundred meter plot of land, or roughly one thousand to one-thousand-three hundred-foot plot. Similar to many of the homes in the neighborhood, ours had a seven-foot wall built all around it and a number of rooms scattered within it. My grandparents had their own room, my mother and I had another, and everyone else in the household shared a large room that doubled as the living room during the day; our kitchen was a separate structure.

At the time, my father was in medical school pursuing his degree to become a doctor. He did not live with us but visited on occasion. Life in Shigla was simple, consisting of nothing other than spending lots of time with family and participating in neighborhood and *Cøllø* community activities every so often. On most days, childhood didn't seem so bad. Yes, we certainly faced many struggles and hardships, but back then it all seemed normal. I did not realize how truly dire our situation was until I began to reflect on my life and early childhood in Sudan and compared it to my experiences in Cairo, Egypt, and later to Buffalo, New York.

Growing up in *Shigla Haj-Yousif* in the early '90s was tough for a number of reasons. First and foremost, we were the first generation of South Sudan children born in the capital, Khartoum, during Sudan's second civil war. The first civil war, Anyanya I, erupted as Sudan was preparing to gain independence in 1956 and continued until 1972, ending with the signing of the Addis Ababa Accords between the central government and the Sudan People's Liberation Army (SPLA). The second civil war, Anyanya II, considered a continuation of the first war between the government and the SPLA, erupted in 1983 and raged on for the next twenty-two years. In 2005, the government and the Sudanese People's Liberation Movement (SPLM), the political wing of the SPLA, signed the Comprehensive Peace Agreement (CPA) designed to end one of the world's longest civil wars. It was a war that killed between two and five million Sudanese, the overwhelming majority being Southerners, and displaced many more from their homes and villages. [2]

In 1989, the year of my birth, Army Brigadier General Omar Al Bashir rose to power following a bloodless military coup de taut. Bashir's ascension to the presidency sought to govern the entire country under Sharia Law, exploiting the southern regions which were rich in resources, marginalizing non-Muslims and ethnic minorities from power, and perpetuating the conflict. For thirty years, Bashir remained in power ruling the country with an iron fist and committed war crimes and crimes against humanity such as the

---

2   "South Sudan Profile – Timeline," *BBC News, Accessed March 5, 2021.*

Darfur genocide and the assault on the Nuba mountains. These civil wars and internal conflicts account for the majority of Sudan's post-independence era and were mostly fought in jungles, swamps, flatlands, and mountainous regions of South Sudan, which devastated the people living in those regions.

Up north in the capital, no one really talked about the war or its effects on the southern population. On occasion, you might have heard the adults talking about family members who were fighting in the war, but it always sounded like something happening in another world far away, not Sudan. Granted I was still a young boy. I was old enough to remember it as one topic no one wanted to discuss. Not my family, my neighbors, or anyone in the community talked about the war. It may have been an attempt to protect us, the young generation of Southerners, from the trauma and devastation of civil war, or to avoid reliving the experience of what it was like to flee their homes for safety.

It's also possible the community of South Sudanese, uprooted from their homes and forced to live in the capital for safety, suffered from a form of collective Post-traumatic stress disorder (PTSD). No one dared to talk about these traumas because it was considered taboo. Sudanese across the board are conservative traditionalists, and both North and South Sudanese typically do not discuss certain emotional or traumatic topics. Instead, most of them dismiss these topics as no big deal, or simply bury them deep down within. Living in a society that paints emotions and vulnerability as an unacceptable sign of weakness, especially for males, inevitably will produce unintentional consequences.

It certainly can be argued many of the negative behaviors in some Sudanese communities can be attributed to often-suppressed emotions and traumas. As a child, I've faced similar challenges and felt pressured to deal with them the same way everyone else around me did. I remember being called a troublemaker for trying to stand up for myself. I remember being called names, disrespected by adults and parents of some school mates, and I remember being treating as an outcast because I didn't come from a perfect family and had a strange name. These instances were traumatic and had a negative effect on my childhood. Although my personal experience is quite different and cannot be compared to those of children fleeing their homes and villages in the war-torn regions of South Sudan, they also had real impacts on my family and me.

CHAPTER 4

American Stories

———

Throughout my childhood, I heard countless stories about life in America. Back then, no one referred to the United States as the US, USA, or anything else; it was always "America!" It was a go-to topic filled with excitement and enthusiasm amongst me and my friends. We talked about America with an imaginary backdrop that read, "Greatest place on Earth." Lots of people, adults and children alike, often shared stories they'd heard from friends or relatives about life in the US and other developed nations. Regardless of where the stories came from, or who shared them, the experience and message was usually the same. There was always a hopeful and cheerful tone to them. You felt a real sense of possibility that one day, in the not-so-distant future, the opportunity to witness and experience life in one of those nations would come to pass. For me, however, my mind was always fixed on the idea of one day visiting America, the "Greatest place on Earth."

I listened to those stories from my friends, their relatives, and sometimes people I didn't know very well visiting relatives in the neighborhood. Hearing their versions of this wildly different reality was fascinating and piqued my curiosity. I paid close attention to everything said and believed every word. Sometimes when my friends were the ones sharing new stories they had recently heard, they would either forget some important details because of their overwhelming level of excitement, or they would knowingly spin the story to make things seem more interesting and mind-blowing. Either way, the rest of us went along down the rabbit hole and believed every word, every time.

There was one story in particular I found to be very interesting, and it was about the roads and streets in America. According to one of my young friends, he heard from a "reliable" source the streets and roads in America were made of gold. I know this may sound absurd, but remember these conversations were among children between the ages of six and eight, maybe nine, before the internet era. To make matters worse, we had no access to magazines, newspapers, posters, or any documents with actual pictures of American cities. There were no images of New York City I recall seeing, and there were no posters or news articles of Washington, DC widely available throughout Sudan.

Imagine life before the smartphone revolution, before everyone you know had a fully functional handheld computer at their disposal. Imagine what life was like before we had the capability to access the world wide web in an instant. With a push of a button, we can now access information on just about any topic in a matter of seconds. We can research current events across the world, access articles about World War II, or check the stock market without having to leave the comfort of our homes. You can now order almost anything on Amazon, eBay, or any of the other online platforms and have it delivered to your door. You can tweet or post your thoughts, pictures, or videos on Facebook, Instagram, and a number of other social media outlets all with a single handheld device.

Ten years ago, the world was a different place with much less technological advances in all those sectors. Twenty years ago, access to information was nothing comparable to today, and any other time before that was basically the dark ages. Now imagine growing up in a part of the world that was much less advanced than the United States and other developed countries. Imagine living in a society where the government controls the media and restricts access to information it deems unfavorable against those in power.

During a period when access to information was largely available through printed news articles and televised and radio broadcast, government action could easily manipulate your entire world view. What you were exposed to through the media and other outlets influenced your perception of what was true and what wasn't. Sudan was one of those restrictive countries and very much still is at this current moment. When access to information across society is restricted and filled with propaganda, it becomes very easy to accept and believe certain ideas, particularly as a child. Suddenly, the idea of golden roads in a land far, far away can seem plausible, especially in America, the "Greatest country on Earth."

The idea of America being a sort of heaven on Earth was perpetuated by the circumstance of our standards of living. Growing up poor meant you were effectively sealed off from consuming American culture, or much of any other popular culture from around the world. I did not grow up watching American movies, TV shows, or listening to American music. But there were iconic hit songs such as "Billie Jean" by Michael Jackson and "I Will Always Love You" by Whitney

Houston that managed to reach just about every remote part of the world. [3], [4] There were also blockbuster movies such as the *Rambo* series starring Sylvester Stallone, *Predator* starring Arnold Schwarzenegger, and *Predator 2* starring Danny Glover. [5], [6] Besides those culturally significant artistic creations, very few other things about America and American pop culture reached us in Sudan.

The main reason was most families in our neighborhood, mine included, did not own a television set. In fact, there were only a hand full of families rich enough to afford a black and white, or even better a colored, TV set. In addition, they also had to have enough money to buy a battery for their TVs to work because there were no electric services offered to our neighborhood.

My grandfather had a small silver radio, given to him as a gift by one of my uncles during his visits. He loved that radio and took it everywhere with him. During the evenings, Grandpa sat in a chair alongside one of the compound walls, usually in the shade to escape the hot sun. There, he listened to world news, and I often sat on the ground next to his feet pretending to understand the news reports. The reports were usually in the English language, most likely from the British Broadcasting Corporation (BBC).

Although I did not understand a word broadcasted over the radio, of course Grandpa understood. I remember the gibberish sounding like a British accent in the reporter's

3   "Billie Jean by Michael Jackson," Song Facts, *Accessed March 5, 2021.*

4   "I Will Always Love You by Whitney Houston," Song Facts, *Accessed March 5, 2021.*

5   Wesley Morris, "1985: When 'Rambo' Tightened His Grip on the American Psyche," *The New York Times, May 30, 2020.*

6   McTiernan, *Predator, 1987.*

voice. It was amusing in a way and a bit funny to my childish ears. But more importantly, I thought of it as one of the most important things Grandpa and I used to do together on a regular basis. It was my special time with him, and no one interfered with it.

I did not become fluent in the English language listening to the evening news with my grandfather unfortunately, nor did I have any real interested in learning the language. I did however manage to become familiar with a few words from those sessions. I learned the English names of major countries, their capitals, and large cities such as London, Paris, Tokyo, and Washington, DC, which was impressive considering my lack of interest in the news. My sole interest was spending time with my grandpa, whom I thought very highly of and adored. So, I sat and listened whenever I had the chance, not to American pop culture and music but to the world news from BBC.

One of my good childhood friends once shared a story he heard from a relative about the lavish lifestyle in America. His relative told him about how all Americans, every single citizen, lived a life of luxury and comfort. The highlight of the story was, "In America, every citizen had more possessions than any of us has ever seen in Sudan, or anywhere else in the world for that matter." He went on to describe how all Americans lived in villas and mansions and drove multiple cars and luxury Jeeps. For my friends and I, the title "Jeep" was used in reference to describe all luxury SUVs regardless of the brand. Anytime we saw a nice SUV drive pass our neighborhood on the main road, someone from the group would usually shout out, "That's my Jeep!" Wishful thinking, of course, given no one we knew actually owned a luxury vehicle, let alone an actual Jeep. It was just a game we played to see which one of us could claim the highest number of nice cars driving past in the distance.

My friend continued to describe the lavish lifestyle all Americans were entitled to and stressed the point each person had access to anything and everything they desired. If someone wanted a new house in America, they simply got it. If they wanted a new car, they got it. If they wanted to travel and go anywhere in the world, they simply boarded a flight and went there. Lastly, he stressed, in America if someone wanted new clothing and new shoes—yes you guessed it—they got it. In fact, he said everyone had so many clothes and shoes no one ever wears the same pair of socks more than once. I was sold.

That was my favorite part of the story, the part where you didn't have to wear a pair of socks twice. Yes, living in a mansion sounded great, the multiple cars too, and the abundance of clothing was also nice. However, never having to wear a pair of socks more than once was the most exciting part, for me at least, because I loved wearing new socks as a child. It's a bit wild to think about, but as a child I rarely got new pairs of socks, and I hated wearing old ones. I remember my mother once bought me a new pair of red socks for Christmas, and I fell in love with them.

They were red, I mean *red*! So bright red they were the first article of clothing anyone noticed on me at Christmas. I had a new outfit to go with them, too: a new light blue button-down shirt and dark colored jeans. I had a pair of black CAT shoes with the iconic white and yellow Caterpillar logo on them, the American construction equipment manufacturer giant. For some reason, they were popular at the time and I was lucky enough to get a pair. It was one of the best Christmases I remember, and I was grateful and very happy that year.

I was old enough and understood the idea of living in a mansion would be amazing, but I'd never been in one. I had seen these big, beautiful homes on TV from Egyptian series and foreign movies, but I never pictured my family and I living in one. I had no real idea of what it felt like to live in a big, nice house, let alone a mansion or villa. I had no idea what it was like to have a car because no one I knew had one. No one in my family owned a single vehicle, let alone multiple cars. In fact, I didn't really know anyone who regularly traveled around town in a private vehicle. If they had access to a vehicle, it was probably through some foreign non-governmental organization (NGO) operating in Sudan at the time, like the United Nations (UN).

Honestly, until we moved to New York, the thought of one day being able to drive a car never crossed my mind. It was considered a luxury good, reserved only for the rich and powerful like government officials, NGOs, and businessmen who could afford it. I also didn't have an abundance of clothes growing up, but I had enough to relate to the idea of having a closet full of everything I needed would be awesome. I thought it was a more realistic concept, similar to the idea of having multiple pairs of socks.

When I first got those red socks for Christmas of 1995 or 1996, I use to tuck my pant legs into those red socks and pull them up as high as possible so they were fully visible. On the days I wore shorts, I made sure the socks were pulled up close to my knees and didn't care about what anyone else thought. I did this for weeks, long past Christmas and well into the new year. Unfortunately, it was only a matter of time before my new socks lost their elasticity, had holes on the bottom, and started to look less red and worn out. I dreaded this moment because I knew it was going to be a while before I got a new pair of socks, and the worst part was they might not be red. But as the saying goes, *Beggars can't be choosers*. So, you see, I think it's completely understandable for a six or seven-year-old boy to be impressed and excited about such prospects in America. I thought the idea of a place where people didn't have to suffer the consequences of not having enough pairs of "red socks" was the best part of life in America and its unbelievably awesome standard of living.

It's embarrassing to admit now, but I was probably more gullible than the other boys growing up. Possibly because I was one of the youngest among my friends, or because I had always had a habit of giving people the benefit of the doubt. It was always easy to believe all the wonderful stories about America, and deep down in my heart I felt I would get the chance to witness it on my own. I had no clue as to how that might actually happen, but I believed it would, nonetheless. I believed it so much, I often visualized and imagined walking through the golden streets of New York City. I would try my hardest to picture what it felt like walking on gold-plated streets with my new shoes and new socks every single day. Yes, I believed New York City had streets made from gold because that's what I was told by a trusted friend once, and also because I was a kid with a wild imagination that has never seen an actual picture of New York City.

I never thought in just a few of years I would actually end up in America staring at the bright ceiling lights at John F. Kennedy International Airport. As gullible as I was, no one could have convinced me to believe my family and I would eventually end up in western New York in some town with a strange name like Buffalo, and terrible freezing weather. It's hard to believe all these major life-changing experiences happened within just a few years from the moment my friends and I spent talking, wondering, and dreaming about one day visiting America. It's mind-blowing. To end up on American soil with my parents and three younger siblings with the opportunity to start a new life and make this country our new home was surreal to say the least. It was a reality I never imagined happening in my wildest dreams.

These memories are near and dear to my heart because they remind me of the good and bad times in Khartoum. They also serve as a window into my childhood and help put certain things about that time period in context. I didn't quite understand a lot of those events, nor did I appreciate the gravity of most of them growing up. Even though I was old enough to understand life was difficult for my family in Sudan, I didn't quite grasp how tough it really was for my parents to provide for us. Now that I'm older, I'm thankful for all they've done and sacrificed for my siblings and I despite the overwhelming challenges we all faced in Khartoum.

**

Christmas was also a time for celebration, and I was always blessed with something new. However, there were two other occasions I normally received new clothes and maybe shoes as well. The first was for school, and the second was for my birthday if I was lucky that year. This was also true for some of my friends and other kids in the neighborhood. Most parents and families would do their absolute best to buy new clothes and shoes for their children, but there were no guarantees. Every kid would look forward to Christmas because they were more likely than not getting new clothes, shoes, and socks. That meant you had to take really good care of those articles of clothing over the holiday season, just in case you were out of luck for your birthday! At least that's what I had to do because my birthday is in March and there was no telling if I would receive anything more besides a "Happy Birthday!"

For the rest of the year, I would try to take excellent care of my clothes, shoes, and especially my socks. I always tried to keep them as clean as possible, despite the often-dusty Khartoum weather. This was partly because my school had a very strict uniform policy and because I also loved looking my best. I attended the Comboni school system along with many of the kids from the neighborhood. The school was named after Saint Daniele Comboni, an Italian Roman Catholic bishop who served as a missionary in Sudan and Africa in the mid-to-late nineteenth century.[7] Typical of Catholic school systems around the world, Comboni schools had very strict uniform polices for all students.

They also had brutal enforcement measures in place too many teachers were happy to employ. Most teachers enforcing uniform and other school policies such as good behavior were "reasonable." However, there were teachers who were merciless and made it clear they were not to be taken lightly in or outside of class. The uniform policy quickly shot up to the top of my list for major things to pay close attention to, and to keep in mind at all times for school.

There were only few other issues I obsessed over during that time period; one was my grades, and the other was the need to remain first or second place on the list of the top five best students in the teachers' classes. I did not know it then, but I became so concerned with being a perfect student I may

---

7   "Daniel Comboni," *Vatican, Accessed March 5, 2021.*

have developed a moderate form of obsessive-compulsive disorder (OCD). Until this very day, I have to press all my clothes and straighten out all the wrinkles or I cannot wear them. I still struggle with the idea of wearing wrinkled clothing, leaving a mess in my room or apartment, or performing a host of simple tasks without near perfect execution. It's extremely difficult sometimes, and the thought alone can be very uncomfortable.

My education has always been a priority for as long as I can remember. When it came to my studies, I was motivated by two things: one, I aimed to be one of the best students in school so I could get excellent grades, graduate at the top of my class, and one day travel to America to continue my studies at the university level. I wanted to have access to the best possible education, so I could achieve my second goal and source of motivation, which was to become a successful professional in my field of study and earn enough to buy my mother a beautiful home. At an early age, I knew I wanted to study medicine and become a doctor just like my father. For a couple of years thereafter, probably between the ages of four and seven years old, I told everyone who would listen my plan was to become a doctor when I grew up.

I was so convinced I had it all figured out, and all I had to do is wait for fate to deal its hand until I was old enough to make it a reality. However, I had one issue to deal with, which was I needed to convince one of my uncles I was serious about my plans for the future to become a doctor. As I mentioned before, our household in Khartoum was filled with relatives who visited for as long as they wished. Some visiting family members stayed with us for short periods of time, and others stayed longer. I always enjoyed having family visit, and it often played out in my favor.

I was the oldest child in the household, and there were perks to having more aunties and uncles around the house. First, they usually were much nicer and more lenient than everyone else, and I appreciated that. When they first arrived, it usually meant gifts and sweets for their oldest nephew, and they would often defend me from getting a whipping for misbehaving. However, this uncle was an exception. He did not bring any gifts or sweets for me when he first arrived and did not live with us for very long either. Unfortunately, before leaving this uncle did manage to seriously derail my hopes and dreams of one day becoming a medical doctor. But my love, drive, and determination to obtain an education lived on and never faded away.

CHAPTER 5

First Day of School

———

I can still remember being anxious and excited about my first day of school. I loved the idea of being in a classroom with my teacher and other students so much I couldn't wait to start kindergarten. I had this crazy idea in mind of what it felt like to be in a classroom with my friends and classmates, and it was super exciting. In reality, I had no idea because I had never been in a school setting before, and what little I knew was based on stories my school-age friends had shared with me. The rest of the details were a product of my wildly overactive imagination.

It was probably around my fourth birthday I began taking a real interest in attending school, but I wasn't yet registered to attend class. I knew it was only a matter of time before I started attending school, and my friends and I all looked forward to it. We hoped to all be at the same school, but none of us knew for certain if that would happen. There were a few primary schools nearby most of the kids I knew attended, and I was sure at least one or two of my mates would end up in the same school with me. Some of my friends had older siblings who were enrolled ahead of us, and so they were our primary source for information about the classroom experience. For me, that was reassuring and gave me some confidence about my own prospects in classroom.

A few months before the start of the school year, I developed a habit of regularly asking the older kids about their school days. It was an attempt to gather as much insight as possible about what to expect when the first day of school finally arrived. I wanted to be prepared and asking questions was the best way I knew how. It was also the easiest part of that process because waiting for enrollment into kindergarten was brutal. At some point I became so eager to start school I would wake up super early, get dressed, and try to follow some of the school-age kids to class. I had many unsuccessful attempts, but I did once manage to blend in with the kids at a local school before the teacher realized I wasn't one of her students.

The school was one of the closest to our home, and I knew a few kids who were students there; one was a girl around my age. She was my neighbor and lived there with her grandmother. One morning I saw her heading off to school and decided to join her and go to her classroom as a visitor. I didn't think it was a big deal, nor did I think it was wrong. So, we walked to her school together and met some of her classmates along the way. Some kids I knew, others I did not, but it was exciting to be a part of this new group of school kids. The commute was about ten minutes from home, and it was a straight shot down one street off the main road near our house.

When we finally made it to the school, I followed the girl and a couple of the kids into their classroom. I made sure to sit next them near the front of the class, and I was ready for whatever came next. At that age, I still had no real idea about how the educational system in Sudan worked. I simply thought students showed up with a pencil and paper and the teachers did the rest. Honestly, that was the only interesting part I had in mind. I simply wanted to be in the classroom with other kids doing whatever it was they did. My goal was to show up and prove I could learn quickly and be an excellent student, more so than any of the other kids on their first day. I wanted to be first, and I didn't want to wait any longer until the next school year to make it happen.

All was well during the beginning of class, and I felt content with how my plan was going so far. I managed to leave home, join a group of neighborhood kids on way their school, and secure a pretty good seat in their classroom, all without get caught or into any trouble that morning. Or so I thought. While in my "new classroom," I couldn't contain my excitement and I couldn't help but try to participate in answering questions the teacher posed to the class. At first, I don't think the teacher noticed I wasn't one of her regular students, or perhaps she may have thought I was a new student assigned to her class. But after a while, she asked my name, and I answered "Olwak." She looked puzzled for a second and asked if my parents brought me to school, and I answered "la" meaning no in Arabic. I continued to *spill the beans* and said, "I came to school today with my friends" and pointed at the girl and some of the other kids as well.

I can tell the teacher was puzzled and didn't know how to react at. She looked shocked at the same time she was trying her best not to burst out with laughter. After a moment, she responded and said, "*Malesh*" meaning I'm sorry in Arabic, "but you cannot simply come to school for the first time on your own without your parents." Then she asked me to go home and come back with my mom or dad. After hearing those words, I was filled with disappointment and slowly got up off my seat and walked out of her class. The walk back home felt like a full day's walk even though it was only about ten minutes way. That was my first and last attempt to rush the process of starting school, and it was heartbreaking.

When I was officially enrolled in school, this time by my mother through the proper channels, I simply couldn't wait for my first day in class. This was roughly six or seven months after my attempt to self-enroll for a day at my friend's school. Part of the reason for my overwhelming excitement was the fact it was customary for all school children to get new school uniforms. I thought the moment I'd been waiting for has finally arrived. I had wanted and even asked for my new school uniform to be purchased in advance, but I had no choice but to wait. But now the wait was over, and I couldn't contain myself. To put things in context, my excitement wasn't necessarily solely about being prepared to officially start school, it was also about the fact I would be receiving new clothes, shoes, and maybe socks for something other than Christmas or my birthday.

Before I became a student officially, Christmas was my favorite holiday and time of the year for more than one reason. It was a time young kids like myself were most likely to receive new outfits and gifts as I mentioned in the third chapter. I always looked forward to it, and I still do today because of the beautiful memories from Sudan. The month of December was always a very special time for us growing up. Not only did we celebrate the birth of Christ, but we also celebrated each other and our cultures. This was common practice for South Sudanese living in the capital, Khartoum, and throughout the country. Most Southerners are a part of the Christian minority community, living in the majority Muslim population of Northern Sudan. Christmas was one of the only times throughout the year we had the opportunity to experience genuine joy and happiness. We also got to create an environment conducive to celebrating our Christian faith. Until my family left Sudan, I always looked forward to Christmas for all its festivities and for the possibility of receiving a special gift or two. But now that I was of school age, I could begin looking forward to the possibility of receiving new school uniforms every year as well.

When I finally got my new school uniform, I remember my level of excitement was through the roof. My mom bought me a short-sleeve, white button-down shirt and navy-blue shorts. I don't exactly remember the shoes I had at the time or whether they were new or not. The memory has slightly faded over the years, but I know I wasn't as excited about the shoes as I was about the new uniform. They may have been a pair of my Christmas shoes I was forced to wear only on special occasions until school started later that year. Nonetheless, I was now a school-aged kid with a new school uniform just like the rest of my friends and some of the neighborhood kids. It was thrilling, and when the first day of school came around, I was the first one up that morning. I was ready to skip breakfast, which was the usual hot tea with a piece of bread. I was ready to run out the door and make my way to class.

The first day at school, I made sure to sit in the first row where I could clearly see the teacher and the chalk board. I wanted an unobstructed view of everything written on the board, and I wanted to hear every question and answer from my new teacher with the utmost clarity. I wanted to also sit where the teacher could see and hear me clearly. My goal on day one was to be very attentive and also ask lots of questions. I probably did, at least more so than some of the other students because I was so excited about finally being in school. There were a couple of reasons I was so eager to learn everything. First, I looked forward to sharing what I learned with everyone at home, especially my grandparents with whom I was close to growing up. The second reason was my competitive nature; I wanted to be the best student in the classroom. My curiosity about essentially everything had always been a driving force throughout my life, even as a young kid. It often served me well and helped me learn about different subjects and topics over the years, but it has also got me into lots of trouble on some occasions.

Following that first day of class, I loved preparing for school every morning. By the time I woke up, my mother usually had my uniform already washed and pressed the night before. She regularly washed my school uniform by hand, my white shirt with *"hebirr"* which was a blue powder widely used for laundry in Sudan. When mixed with clean water, it changed white clothing to a light blue color, the color my uniform needed to be for school. It was a temporary transformation that required repetition with every wash. I often watched Mom wash and press my clothes, and it wasn't very long before I took responsibility for my own school clothes. I mostly wanted to help her, but I also wanted to feel a sense of independence to satisfy my "do it yourself or can do attitude". I liked the feeling, and I quickly picked up the habit of washing my own clothes and ironing everything I wore.

Luckily for me, my first school was located just minutes from our house. I had a few friends who attended the same school, which was great. Most of us were in the same grade, and everyone walked to and from school together. Naturally, we developed our network of friendship more and more, and eventually came up with a system of making sure we returned home on time every day after school. There were two reasons for that. One, each of us needed to go change out of our school clothes, and two, we needed to do so in a timely manner so we could meet up to play before dinner time.

CHAPTER 6

Troubled Child

———

In the first chapter, I explained the name *Shufto* is quite unusual by any standard, and worse, it made life very difficult growing up in *Shigla, Haj Yousif.* In fact, I found myself in lots of trouble because of it. I knew early on I was a curious child by nature, more so than most children, and loved asking questions. I didn't ask questions simply for the sake of asking questions, but because I genuinely wanted answers to my questions. *It's normal for young kids to ask adults question they don't know answers to,* I thought. However, I could not figure out why I got into trouble often for acting like a normal child. Whenever I was interacting with adults and asking questions, making statements, or responding to them, often I was told, "You're being disrespectful" and told I had a smart mouth. With the name *Shufto,* that opinion seemed to quickly circulate around town, and before long it felt as if the entire neighborhood was against me. Overnight, the child with the strange name became everyone's favorite scapegoat, demand child, and black sheep. Imagine thinking that about yourself as a child.

In my mind, the problem wasn't necessarily that I was a bad kid, disrespectful, or because my behavior was out of the ordinary. At least, no more than any other child my age. I was being mistreated as result of my weird name. The name *Shufto* was to blame for all my problems. It was an unpleasant spotlight on me I did not ask for, nor did I understand why my mother picked it. I was angry with my mom about it, and at times felt resentful toward her. I blamed her for painting an unnecessary target on my back, and worse, a curse I could never shake off for the rest of my life.

The name posed an internal conflict within me that was difficult to deal with because I loved my mother and I knew she also loved me very much. But I didn't and could not understand the reasoning or justification for naming me *Shufto*, which brought me nothing but pain. I often asked her about it, sometimes over and over again. I would begin by asking, "Mama, why did you name me *Shufto*?" Before she answered, I would often ask follow up questions such as, "Why would you name me something so unusual? Do you see how everyone makes fun of me? Is that what you want, for your son to be laughed at and made fun of by the entire neighborhood?" She laughed it off sometimes and tried to calm me down because of how worked up and distraught my reactions were about the subject. My episodes became so routine, at one point my mother knew from the look on my face as I walked into the courtyard there was trouble. Of course, it didn't help I was most likely yelling, screaming, and filled with rage. Those actions usually meant something went wrong, an incident most likely involving the name *Shufto*.

Often, trouble seemed to follow home after school, find me at our makeshift playground, and sometimes around the corner near my friend's house. Directly outside our home, there was a huge ditch that had been there for as long as I could remember. It was probably there when I was born, and it remained there untouched years later when my family left Khartoum for Cairo. The ditch was approximately four or five feet wide, and no more than three and a half feet in depth. As a kid I used to walk carefully around its edges so I wouldn't fall in it. It seemed much wider and deeper in my eyes, and it was sometimes pretty scary, particularly during the rainy season. It would often fill up with muddy water, and I dreaded the thought of accidentally falling in and not being able to get out. The most impressive thing about the ditch was its seemingly never-ending length. It appeared to stretch for a distance in both directions past my neighborhood. It was essentially a border for my friends and I that kept us from venturing out too far from home.

Unfortunately for us, everyone who lived in close proximity to ditch seemed to use it as a land fill. People tossed out all sorts of trash in it, and when rain fell, it was a very unpleasant sight. There were no houses or structures built past the ditch; there was simply a massive empty lot situated directly across from our home. The empty space stretched all the way to the main road, "One street" or "*Sharie Wahid.*" That space became our home turf for almost every activity because it was the perfect playground for my friends and me.

We had a list of games we loved to play and football (soccer) was chief among them. Soccer was our go-to sport, and we played it almost every day after school. There were no parks, patches of grass, or much greenery of any kind nearby, nor were there many designated areas for playing in our neighborhood. Outside of the school yard, we had to find and create a safe space on our own to play in. Fortunately for my friends and I, we had our desert soccer field nearby. The main road was a distance away, and the ditch was often dry throughout the year, so we were safe playing there.

Nonetheless, there were a few obstacles we had to overcome: 1) the blazing sun that often burned the soles of our feet, 2) the small rocks and pebbles littered on the ground, and 3) the difficulty of trying to play soccer with no shoes and a makeshift homemade ball.

We usually started our games after school around 2:30–3:00 p.m. First, everyone went home to change out of their school uniform. I would always make it a point to drink cold water from the *zeer*, a water cooler made of red clay. We did not have a refrigerator at home, but the cold water from the *zeer* was very refreshing, especially during the hottest days. This became our daily routine during school days because none of us dared make it to the soccer pitch without first going home to change. If you did not, it basically guaranteed there would be an unpleasant whipping waiting for you at home for playing around in your uniform after school. The audacity to kick a soccer ball with your school shoes was considered to be an even worst offense. It was forbidden. Most of my friends learned that lesson the hard way, but I took their word for it and quickly fell in line. So, you made sure to go home first, change out of those clothes, and came to the pitch with your *safinjat* or sandals, assuming you had a pair to wear or borrow. If you did not have a pair, and if you weren't able to sneak out with someone else's *safinjat*, then your only option was to walk over barefooted.

In either case, it did not matter much because at the end of the day we all ended up playing soccer barefoot. The reason being none of us owned a pair of regular soccer shoes or cleats. First, there was no need for a pair of cleats when there was no grass or artificial turf to play on, and second, we couldn't afford a pair of either footwear. In hindsight, it would have been nice to have a pair of flat soccer shoes to protect our feet from the rocks and hot sun. In addition, the boys who did play wearing a pair of *safinjat* also ended up playing barefoot alongside the rest of us. They put them aside or next to the large rocks we used as goal posts. No one played with their *safinjat* because they would be damaged pretty quickly, and everyone knew sandals are not exactly designed for sport. The only option was to play barefoot and learn to tolerate the blazing heat underneath your feet.

There were some days during midsummer when it was just unbearable to play soccer barefoot. The ground would be so hot, the sight of heat waves rising from the ground was enough to deter anyone thinking about being outside. Any attempt to place your barefoot on the sandy ground was a huge mistake. On those days, my friend and I would choose other games to play like marbles, or build miniature car figurines from old canisters. We often did this in the shade underneath a large tree or in some other shaded areas in the neighborhood. However, those were just ways of killing time while we waited to go back out on the soccer field. In the early morning hours or evenings during the summer, the sun was usually bearable. During those times, my group of friends and I would meet at the playground with our makeshift soccer balls and choose one for the game. Whichever most of us agreed to be the best homemade soccer ball was the game ball that day.

We did not have an Adidas, Nike, or any other manufactured soccer ball with a logo growing up. It may be difficult to imagine playing soccer without an actual soccer ball, but we made it work. It would have been amazing if one of the kids from our group had a real ball, but the reality was a buying one was quite expensive and none of our parents were rich enough to afford it. They considered it to be a toy for rich kids, and we were not among that group. So, no one bothered to ask for one. Instead, we made our own soccer balls using a sock and stuffed it with paper and plastic bags. The end-product was a semi-roundish sock ball. It often had hardly any bouncing ability depending on the paper to plastic bag ratio. If there was more paper, less bounce, and if there were more plastic bags, more bounce that made it easier and better for juggling.

I reminisce about those days on occasion and remember the laughter and smiles on my friends' faces. I think about the fact we played with a ball made from things most people consider to be trash. I also remember having to use rocks and whatever else we could find nearby as goal posts, the pain shooting up my leg after accidentally kicking one of the rocks trying to score a goal, and fearlessly going in for a defensive tackle barefooted. I would often hobble home with a bloody toe and try to hide it from my mom so she wouldn't get upset and yell at me for being careless. Or worst, she would force me to stay home for more than a few days even after I'd convinced myself my injury was fully and miraculously healed.

The troubling moments as well as the good and fun-filled times with my friends both make up an integral part of my childhood. They are an essential part of my identity and who I was growing up in Khartoum. They are important parts of my early life experience not only because I can look back and remember my home and birthplace, but because I've grown to understand and see their value. Naturally, it's much easier to recall and reflect on the nostalgic moments compared to traumatic ones. However, all those memories and many others have helped me learn and appreciate so much more during various points in life outside of Sudan. I still often rely on them for perspective, even at this very point of my life as an adult man living halfway across the world from my old neighborhood of *Shigla, Haj Yousif.*

CHAPTER 7

Lasting Impressions

It's vital and important to recognize some childhood experiences have a lasting effect. Not all, but most people have a set collection of childhood memories that have had a significant impact on their lives. Some memories may serve as a healthy foundation for the building blocks of someone's character, and others may be the root cause of someone else's worst impulses. Regardless of the outcome, profound childhood memories and experiences can have serious and lifelong impacts on just about anyone. Those experiences may be unique to each and every person, and they may not all be memories of joy. They certainly may not all be of fulfilled moments with family and friends, but they will always be a part of our history. What matters most is what we make of them moving forward in life.

I often focused on the moments I spent with my friends running around and pretend fighting on our playground as a kid, the moments spent arguing over penalty kicks, foul calls, and accusations of unsportsmanlike conduct. Those moments are what helped make growing up in Sudan special and worthwhile in its own unique way. After all, what truly mattered to us as kids was that we had each other. We had a strong bond of friendship and brotherhood that helped us to make the best of a difficult childhood, especially for a kid like myself. I chose to hold on to and cherish the good moments because they brought me joy, and I dealt with the bad ones the best way I knew how. Throughout my childhood and well into my adolescence, I looked for ways to keep moving forward, kept pushing ahead, and never let anyone or anything hold me back. It wasn't always easy, and I didn't always know what do to, but that did not keep me from trying to make the best of my situation.

Most people would agree and can relate that we all have had to face some personal challenges as kids. Whether it was difficulty making new friends at school, or dealing with bullies, we all had to face those challenges and figure out a way to overcome them. This was no different for me. But some of my personal challenges went beyond playground drama. It sometimes felt like I was trapped with no way out, and there were moments when things got so bad, I simply couldn't figure out what to do.

What made matters worse was I was no longer dealing with just the kids in my neighborhood teasing me about my name. I also had to figure out how to deal with adults and people I considered to be family and friends at a young age. It was a nightmare and a daily struggle, but over time I learned to deal with the jokes and unpleasant comments from random people I didn't know. I would try my best to simply dismiss them in my mind and pretend I didn't hear a word. However, with family or friends, at some point it became unbearable and too difficult to look the other way. It felt like betrayal. It felt mean-spirited, disrespectful, and deeply hurtful. I couldn't understand why my own family and friends would do that to me. Whenever that happened, I got angry and began to lash out.

There were two specific instances I remember pushing me far over the edge. The first involved one of my relatives, my uncle who I referenced in the fourth chapter. I mentioned he loved joking about my plans to become a medical doctor. He came to live with us for a brief period in my grandparents' home when I was about six or seven years old. At first, he seemed fine, and I had no issues having him around, but I quickly learned he was no average uncle. I learned his favorite hobby was making jokes and thought of himself as an aspiring comic, which was fine by me. The only problem I had with his material was I was often the punch line. I was his go-to subject, and he loved joking about me and my name, *Shufto*, which I did not laugh about or find particularly funny or amusing.

By that point I was aware my father was working on his medical degree, and I was in love with the idea of medicine. I liked the thought of being a doctor so much I started to tell everyone, "When I grow up, I'm going to become a doctor just like my father." For a while after that, I was fully convinced my destiny was to save lives through medicine. However, I started losing confidence in that idea when my comedic uncle turned it into a game and started teasing me about it. He would start laughing whenever I talked about being a doctor and even started to call me a chicken doctor. I argued with him about it at first and demanded he stop calling me chicken doctor immediately! I insisted he accept the fact I was destined to become a "normal doctor," a doctor for human beings and nothing else. My understanding of what doctors did back then, real doctors like my dad was studying to become, was to treat people. I did not know there were doctors for animals, especially chickens, and to call me one was an insult. I'd never seen or heard of a veterinarian before then, and to me the concept seemed farfetched. Every time my uncle joked about it, I felt more insulted because I didn't believe animals suffered illness like people to the point of needing medical treatment from a doctor.

In a society where few people had household pets, it was unlikely for most kids my age at the time to learn much about veterinary medicine. My uncle didn't exactly explain veterinarians were real professional medical providers, nor did he say it was legitimate branch of medicine. It's possible he did not know either because the handful of doctors we knew all treated people. Instead of using it as an opportunity for a teaching moment, he made a running joke of it that drove me crazy. Because he was my uncle and a grown up, even though he wasn't acting like it, I tried my best not to react negatively on multiple occasions. I couldn't lash out because it was disrespectful and unacceptable, and I was at a point where I had exhausted all options. I needed to find a way to get through to him and get him to understand I was serious about the issue and he needed to stop. Crying about it would not have worked and would be a sign of weakness, and I was taught boys had to be tough and never emotional.

There was only one course of action left that might work with a high likelihood of success. That action was to abandon the idea of medicine once and for all and make it clear to my uncle and everyone else I no longer wanted to be a doctor. I thought, surely, he would stop with the jokes and name calling, and the rest of the household would have nothing else to laugh about, at least not at my expense. To make sure they all knew I meant it, I planned on making it clear I would no longer speak about becoming a doctor. I planned to clarify the point in no uncertain terms that I, Olwak Samuel Ayok Adok-Kack, no longer wanted to pursue medicine in any of its forms as a viable career path when I grow up.

To prove my point and show I meant every word, and to show I hated my uncle for repeatedly making jokes about my dreams to be a doctor, and to get the message across that he was to blame for calling me "doctor chicken," I went to him directly. I said to him, "All this time you've been making fun of me and don't want to listen, so from this day forward I don't want to be a doctor anymore, and I will never study medicine in my life!" I remember the rage I felt right before I spoke those words. Since that moment, never again did I think about or contemplate the idea of becoming a medical doctor. Ever since that point I lost complete interest in the idea of medicine.

When I think about the incident, I wonder what went through my uncle's mind and through the minds of the other family members there. I wondered if they knew I truly meant every word, or if they simply thought I was just being dramatic. My uncle probably did not intent to bruise my six-year-old ego, and he probably also did not mean to cause any harm. I know he did not harbor any ill will toward his young nephew and he probably did not think of it as anything more than just fun and games. If he thought I might take it all to heart I'm sure he would have stopped long ago. Certainly, if he was aware those jokes and name calling might have lasting impacts on me, no doubt he would have stopped the first time I asked him.

In any case, what's done is done and I've learned to live with it. But for a long time before that, I blamed my uncle for derailing my six-year-old "well thought-out plan" for my future. I had it all figured out that once I finished my primary and secondary education, made it to college and completed medical school, I would finally be able to afford to buy my mother a nice house. When and where? I didn't quite think ahead that far at the time. The moral of the story is words have meaning, and words can have serious consequences as well, unintended or otherwise. Make sure to choose your words wisely and be careful what you say to someone, especially a child.

The second occasion I felt disrespected and truly insulted was when our neighbor made a hurtful comment about my mother and me. Those words were unforgettable and deeply insulting. The saddest part about that incident was hearing those words from someone I held in similar regard to my mother. She was no stranger, and I'd known her and her family for years. She had a big family with lots of children, including a young son my age. He and I were good friends, and I thought of him as one of my closest friends, if not my best friend. We spent lots of time together during and after school, but that relationship changed. I blamed him for instigating the events leading to that incident. What I did was wrong, and I was aware of it. I knew I shouldn't have reacted toward him the way I did, but I was convicted it was all his fault.

The day started off normal like any other school day. I woke up early as usual for breakfast, went out into the courtyard just after sunrise, and began brushing my teeth. I then prepared for school and came back out for breakfast. My mother had hot tea and bread ready as usual, and I enjoyed it while chatting away with my grandparents and other family members just waking up. Before I knew it, it was time to run out the door and join my friend and other school kids who normally walked with us to school. Nothing was unusual about that morning and everything seemed to indicate we had a good day ahead.

Our school schedule consisted of early morning assembly in a large courtyard, multi-curriculum classes, and lunch and recess before dismissal. My friends and I usually gathered in the same area daily during lunch and recess to play and hang out while planning our after-school actives. The routine was straight forward because our options were limited to just a hand full of activities and games. We opted to meet up for a game of soccer after school that day, which was surprising to no one, and I was super excited about it. I had been practicing a few new soccer moves on my own and I wanted to show them off during the game. We parted ways after lunch and went back to our respective classrooms for the last few subjects before dismissal.

In class, I found myself anxiously waiting for the final bell to ring for dismissal. I was looking forward to running home right after the bell, changing, and being the first player on the soccer field right outside my door. While still in class, however, the teacher began to notice my unusual behavior. He noticed I wasn't paying attention and seemed uninterested in the subject matter. He wasn't very happy about that. Normally I was well behaved, attentive, and often participated. I regularly asked and answered questions and sitting at the front row made it easier to notice what type of student I was. But on that particular day, I didn't participate or do any of the usual things.

My mind was simply elsewhere, and my anxious behavior was becoming distracting in class. After a few attempts to get me to focus, the teacher decided enough was enough, and I needed to be disciplined since his verbal warnings seemed to fall on deaf ears. He felt the need to make an example out of me, and that's exactly what he did. He called me out of my seat and to the front of the class. Immediately I knew I was in big trouble. I knew what was to follow because I've seen other kids called up, and it never ended well for any of them. The teacher did not say a word once I reached the front of the class, which was just a few feet from my seat. He pulled out the whip, and all I could do after that was try my best not to cry. I remember that whipping very well because it was one of the first, and probably my last, whippings I got in a classroom.

When it was finally time for dismissal, I was the first one out the door. I didn't say anything to anyone, not a word, and kept quiet all the way home. Along the way, my "best" friend and a few other kids who planned on meeting up for a soccer match after school started teasing me about what happened in class. I knew it was going to happen because words travel around fast among students, and it was my first whipping, so I saw it coming. I didn't like that it happened, but I knew it was bound to happen to most students at least once or twice. For me, however, I prided myself on being a good student and trying to avoid those mistakes as much as possible, but on that day, I simply couldn't escape it.

The walk home was dreadful and seemed to take much longer than usual. What made matters worse? My best friend seemed to be the main instigator. Everyone else made a few jokes and moved on, but he would not let go of the topic. He continued mocking me even after everyone else stopped. I kept my silence about the matter, kept walking toward home, and focused on the soccer match ahead. I knew thinking about the game would help me forget about what happened in school, if not completely than at least for some time while having fun with my buddies. My goal was to show off those new moves I'd been practicing for a while, and that was all I wanted to think about.

When I finally made it home, I quickly changed out of my school clothes, took a drink of cold water, and went to the soccer field. As expected, I was the first one there, which was normal because my house was closest. I began setting up the soccer goals using the largest pieces of rocks I could find and cleared out some of the pebbles and small rocks on the field. Shortly after, some of the boys arrived and helped finish clearing the field of any other debris we could find. This was a regular part of our routine to ensure nobody got hurt trying to kick the ball or ended up stepping on a sharp and harmful object. My best friend finally arrived, and he was dressed and ready for the game. By then we had enough players to form two teams and kick off the match.

From the start of the game, it was clear everyone came ready to play. The level of competition was intense right off the bat, and no player seemed to hold back. This wasn't strange because whenever we watched major professional soccer matches like the World Cup, we spent days and sometimes weeks consumed by it and pretending to be our favorite player. We then worked on trying to learn and master new moves like professional footballers. That is, until the next big thing in the football world came around.

Back then during the '90s, access to major professional soccer leagues was very limited in Sudan. We couldn't watch the English Premier League with top teams like Manchester United, Liverpool, Manchester City, Chelsea, and Arsenal play. Nor were we able to follow the Spanish La Liga's El Clasico match where powerhouse Real Madrid, my favorite team, and fierce rival Barcelona went head-to-head. Also, the Italian League A with Juventus, Lazio, AC Milan, Inter Milan, and the German Bundesliga with Bayern München, Borussia Dortmund, and Bayer Leverkusen were nowhere to be found. The French Ligue 1 with Paris Saint-Germain, AJ Auxerre, AS Monaco, and Olympique Lyon were so limited we didn't know much about them at the time.

The FIFA World Cup was all we talked about, especially during the years it took place. I remember watching my first World Cup in 1994 when Brazil won the cup against Italy in a 3-2 penalty shootout. This was my first introduction to Brazilian football, and I loved it. [8] Four years later during the 1998 World Cup, I decided Ronaldo Luís Nazário de Lima, also known as Ronaldo, was my favorite player after watching his performance throughout the tournament. [9] Although the 1998 World Cup final ended in a disappointing loss against the French national team, I enjoyed watching the Brazilian national team defend the Cup against some of the world's best footballers.

That year, every kid in the neighborhood had an alter ego matching their favorite player, and pick-up soccer was filled with more energy and enthusiasm than usual. The quality of football was nothing like the pros of course, and we knew it. We knew it was nowhere close to standards set by professional players on TV, but we didn't really care much about that. After all, they were the best of the best in the world, and we were just local kids in a part of the world most people knew little about.

The energy was very high and similar to the days we played soccer following a World Cup match, or other major football matches. We all acted as if we had something to prove to one another. My best friend and I were pretty competitive by nature, and on any typical day it was obvious.

---

8   "1994 FIFA World Cup USA," *FIFA, Accessed March 5, 2021.*

9   "1998 FIFA World Cup FRANCE," *FIFA, Accessed March 5, 2021.*

However, on that hot and sunny afternoon, our competitiveness reached new heights and turned from friendly to a rivalry.

Normally he and I played on the same team, but not that day. We ended up on opposing teams, and the built-up tension from earlier in day did not help the situation. The fact he kept teasing and coming after me, laughing and joking about the incident in class with the teacher, only added fuel to the fire. I wasn't necessarily still angry with him, but I was growing frustrated with his aggressive and reckless playing style during the match. It was strange and out of character for him to play the way he was playing against everyone, but me in particular. We all knew the risk we posed to one another playing barefooted with no protective gear. There was basically an unspoken rule, and everyone respected it: avoid making overly aggressive challenges on all players, defensive, offensive, and especially (goalkeepers) goalies. There was no need to risk injuring each other and taking someone out of the game.

My friend seemed to ignore the unspoken rule time and time again. He continued to play recklessly against my teammates and I, even after we warned him multiple times. It was completely odd, and we all wondered what his problem was. My teammates and I asked him to take it easy, his own teammates insisted he relax as well, but no one was able to get through to him. Naturally, the flow of the game changed as a result of his hostility against my team. We were all having fun at the start of the game, and everyone had a chance to show off some of their new skills, myself included. But the mood quickly changed as the game went on, and everyone blamed my friend for ruining the game. He did not react well to the criticism from both his teammates and mine. His reaction toward me was the most negative. Once again, he brought up the topic of my school whipping and started laughing and teasing me about my name, *Shufto*.

All my friends knew I was sensitive about the name, and they usually knew when to stop joking about it. They knew it was upsetting, but I also knew what buttons to push in response to keep them from going too far. I would always try to downplay their lame old jokes and insist I'd heard it all before. My best friend happened to be in a world of his own and seemed intent on causing problems with everyone, especially me. We all tried our very best to continue playing before it was dinner time, which usually meant time to come in for the night. Having had enough, we all decided it was best to end the match after the next goal and try again the day after without my friend. To no one's surprise, he did not like the idea of being excluded from the group very well. He really didn't like my suggestion he should stay away until he was ready to play ball without the drama.

At that very point an argument erupted between me and him, and not long after, a fight broke out. I can't recall exactly what he said to me during the argument, but my reaction was to pick up the nearest item next to me and throw it at him. At the time, I did not know what it was I picked up, but it wasn't a homemade sock ball stuffed with plastic and paper. I wished and hoped it was, but what I grabbed from the ground was instead a solid item. Immediately after I threw it, I heard a loud scream from my friend. The next sight in front of me was him with his hands covering his forehead and blood beginning to flow through his fingers.

My heart sank, and I felt an intense and horrible feeling inside my chest about the crime I had just committed against my best friend. Immediately, I tried to apologize and explain

I didn't know it was a rock I picked up—not just any rock, but one of the large rocks we used as a goal post. I yelled about it having been an accident. I didn't mean to hurt him and I especially did not mean to hit him on the head. I was just upset about everything that happened on and off the pitch, and nothing more.

He probably did not hear anything I said because he was in so much pain. Some of boys froze where they stood, and a few tried to calm him down and reassure him the injury did not look as severe as it might have felt. After a few minutes, we were able to finally convince him to remove his hands from his forehead so we could examine the damage. It looked probably as bad as it felt, if not worse. I knew I was in big trouble and there was nothing I could do or say to wiggle my way out of this situation. I knew right then and there what was to follow would be extremely unpleasant—the reaction from my mother for this horrible act against someone else's child, and from my friend's mother for harming her son.

My friend's mother was a big lady, both in physical stature and character. She was big and tall, and throughout the neighborhood everyone knew it was best to avoid getting on her bad side. I personally was well aware of that fact because I had seen my friend deal with the repercussions of upsetting his mother. Everyone in his household feared her more than they feared their father. I knew it was only a matter of time before she showed up at our house looking for me. After the terrible incident, when we all decided to part ways, the guys pitied me as they walked away. They feared what might happened to me once my friend got home and his mom discovered I was the responsible culprit behind the violent act. They had every right to be, and I was more afraid than all of them combined. As we all feared, but to no one's surprise, his mother was at our front door and into the courtyard not long after my friend got home.

When she burst into our house, my mother and everyone in the house knew there was trouble. They just did not know exactly what kind of trouble they were about to deal with. The family also knew more than likely it had something to do with me. They suspected I probably did something I shouldn't have and didn't want discovered because of the way I came into the house minutes before her arrival. I walked in quietly and tried to keep my presence unknown for as long as I possibly could, but to no avail. Someone saw me sneaking in. It was news to me, but whenever I came home quiet and trying not to be noticed, it was a clear indication I had probably done something wrong. My family already figured out I was attempting to avoid what was to follow, but there was no way out.

From her fiery eyes and the look on her face, my friend's mom was clearly agitated. As soon as she stormed in, the usual customary greetings went out the window. It was apparent she did not come over to waste any time. It was clear she had no interest in making small talk with my mother, nor with anyone else for that matter, and she definitely wasn't looking for a simple apology.

"*Shufto wan?*" meaning, "Where is *Shufto?*" she yelled. From the sound of her voice, I thought she was going to kill me for sure. My mom was the first one to respond in her classic calm and concerned voice, and said, "*Fi shuno?*" meaning, "What's going on?" and then said, "*Malo issaaj da?*" meaning, "What's all this noise about?"

My friend's mom quickly responded and insisted—no, demanded—I be brought out in front of her so she could address me directly. At this point my mother still had no idea what happened. She wondered why this woman could not contain her fury against a little boy. The family knew she wasn't the calmest person in the world, but they had never seen her this angry before, toward me or anyone else, not even the last time when she came to our house to complain about her expensive glass window I accidentally broke. That time, I was trying to strike a pigeon with my new homemade slingshot next to her house but missed the bird and broke one of her windows. Obviously, I didn't mean to do it, but she wasn't happy about it and came to complain directly to my mother.

She asked my mother, "What am I to do with your son? I can't ask you to pay for a replacement window because if I did, you can't afford it. I see you struggling to take care of your family and to feed your children, so what am I to do?" I was standing next to my mother when the lady spoke those words to her. I saw in real time how hard she took those comments; I saw it looking at my mom's face. She was silent and did not respond and instead remained quiet until the lady walked away. Had those been her last words to my mother, it may have been slightly more bearable, but they were not. I understood she was upset back then and maybe she had every right to be, but it was nothing like how she was this time around about her kid. She was furious.

With the previous incident fresh in the back of her mind, my mother tried to calm the lady down to avoid another episode. She invited her to have a seat and offered hot tea so they may discuss the problem. She refused. All the while, I could hear the commotion from my hiding spot behind one of the rooms in the house. After a few minutes of back and forth between my mother and our neighbor, they called me out of hiding and forced me to show myself. Once again, my heart sank just like earlier after I hurled the rock at my friend and saw how bad I messed up. This time, however, I felt sympathy for myself and hoped and prayed I didn't end up in bad shape like my friend, or even worse, dead.

Thinking back, I genuinely feared getting the worst whipping known to man from our neighbor. My mom used words more than anything, so I wasn't too concerned about her, but my friend's mother used both words and whips. She also had a reputation for having a heavy hand. After my mother called out a few times, I managed to garner the courage needed to step out from my hideout and face the music. I was afraid of what might happen to me, but I still managed to walk up to both my mom and the neighbor lady. My mind was blank and my heart filled with fear. I thought about the last time I was in similar position, when I broke the window, and thought I was lucky for not getting whipped. In reality, what ended up happening turned out to be much, much worse, not necessarily for me, but for my mother.

While thinking about it, I vividly recalled hearing what she said, how she said it, and wondering why my mother looked so hurt after the fact. I thought about what she might say or do this time, and wondered exactly what she meant the last time when she said what she said to my mother and me. I didn't and couldn't figure it out then, and it took many more years before I understood what her words meant. When I finally did, I realized it was a cruel thing to say to a child and that's why my mother was so insulted.

Those words were, "Ana ma-bareif omik shaf shunu lamin uw wiledic, lakin ma-con ashan-nass-kullo ya shufo!" After speaking those words in Arabic, the lady turned her back and walked away. I remember the look on my mother's face at that moment. It was heartbreaking to see how insulted she was, and

I couldn't help but feel sorry for her. At the time I still didn't quite understand what the lady meant, but my mom clearly did. What she said roughly translated to, "I don't know what your mother saw when she gave birth to you, but it was not meant for everyone else to see." From an outsider's perspective, those words may not seem to be a big deal or much of an insult, but for us there is a much deeper meaning behind them. To say something like that about someone's child is unforgivable.

In Cøllø (Shilluk) culture, one word can have multiple meanings depending on the context. Although they were spoken in Arabic, I knew my mother interpreted them in both languages. I understood she was deeply insulted by them, and I immediately blamed myself for it. My mother meant and means everything to me, and to see someone disrespect her in front of me for something I had done was disheartening.

That incident was still fresh on my mind, and I was afraid this second situation would lead to a similar outcome or worse. I did not want my mom going through the same scenario and end up insulted once again. I had done something much worse this time around by harming my friend and hitting him on the head with a rock. His mother's initial reaction seemed to indicate she was intent on making sure there was a higher price to pay this time around. Based on how angry she was the moment she walked in through our front door, I anticipated the worst possible outcome: a combination of insults and whippings befitting of the crime I had committed against her son. Last time I broke an expensive glass window, and this time I injured her baby boy. The only thing I hoped was for my mother to be spared from facing any consequence for my reckless actions. I did not want her to be disrespected or insulted for what I did.

Luckily, the lady was so upset with me all her focus fell squarely on my shoulders. She yelled at me for a while but decided not to raise a hand. She seemed so dismayed and unsure of a proper punishment for me, after yelling and screaming her lungs out she simply shook her head and went home. In all honesty, I was terrified until the moment she walked away, and even then, I feared she might return to finish the job after a while. Thankfully, she did not. However, those two experiences lead me to become more protective of my mother. I tried my very best after that moment to never put her in a similar position again. I can't say I miraculously transformed into the perfect son or a model citizen, but I did try my absolute best until the day we left Sudan for Egypt.

CHAPTER 8

My Mother and I

My relationship with my mother is a special and unique one with many layers. As her first born son, I always felt a sense of obligation to be there for her and to be her little helper in any capacity. That sense of responsibility manifested in different ways throughout my life, and over time it became more and more meaningful. The older I grew, the more obligated I felt to be there for her. Throughout my childhood in Khartoum, especially around the age of eight through ten, I was conscious of that fact. At first, I thought of it as nothing more than simply being a good kid, but deep down inside I genuinely believed it was my role as her firstborn son.

Part of the reason I developed a strong and close relationship with my mother was because my father wasn't around much growing up, and she was my only parent. The other part was cultural and based on what I saw as a male's role in the household. As a child, I didn't know much about the nature of my parent's relationship and I didn't know why they were apart. It was clear my dad wasn't around often, but I did not understand why he and Mom were not together in the same household like most of my friends' parents. All I knew was my father came around on occasion to visit. Whenever he did, I was only permitted to spend a short amount of time with him before he was gone once again. On some of those visits, he treated me for malaria or whatever illness I was dealing with at the time. During those moments, I always went to see him at my auntie's home, but he never came over to see me at my grandfather's home where Mom and I lived. During one of those visits, I discovered he was studying to be a medical doctor, and for years after it became my understanding for why dad was always gone.

I was raised in a traditionally conservative environment with certain values instilled in me from a young age. I learned early on and understood men and women have defined roles in the household, and each gender had a set of obligations to fulfill on a regular basis. The men in the house—my grandfather, stepfather, and uncles—were all providers. They were obligated to work and earn a living to the support the family. The women—my grandmother, my mom, and aunts—were responsible for cooking, cleaning, and taking care of the children. I saw this family structure as the norm not only in my house, but also in other homes in the neighborhood such as my aunt's house.

My father had a younger sister who lived minutes away from us. Whenever he visited, my father stayed at her home with her and her family. Growing up, I spent most of my time in her household. She had two sons close to my age, and we grow up together like siblings. I was basically a middle child between the two of them; one was older by a year, the other was younger by a year, and we were all inseparable. Growing up in both households essentially informed and solidified my understanding of what it meant to be a good son to my mother, and what I thought every boy needed to do if they wished to one day be a responsible man.

The two families were emblematic of most household structures in our Cøllø community, as well as many other Sudanese communities. Sudanese culture, like most cultures in African and around the world, revolves around a communal way of life. Most people in Sudan live in multigenerational households with grandparents, parents, and children coexisting in one household. My family is a perfect example because my mother and I lived in my grandparents' household throughout all of my childhood. We had many family members living with us for years, and others visiting for shorter periods of time. It is common practice to regularly accept more people into the household because of the widely accepted notion family is family, and they are welcomed. In my culture in particular, it is the norm to welcome relatives and family friends into our homes. Usually, no family was turned away, and that was my experience throughout childhood in Khartoum.

My mother was very protective over me as a child, and I didn't quite realize it until my teenage years. She and I began having conversations reminiscent of our lives back home. I had very few early childhood memories about life in Khartoum, and I was interested in learning more about our former life in Africa. We did not have a huge photo album full of baby and family pictures, nor did we have home video recordings documenting those years. There was nothing to show the first time I started crawling, nor the first time I stood on my own two feet. No videos showed my first steps, nor the sound of voice when I spoke my first words in Cøllø and Arabic.

We had to rely almost entirely on my mother's recollection and the very few photos she managed to safeguard over the years. It was sometimes very difficult to imagine the events

Mom illustrated actually happening, and I would rack my brain trying to remember them. During those conversations, I would often ask her repeatedly to describe a single event over and over again, hoping and praying it would spark a memory in my mind. Sometimes her multiple descriptions helped, other times it did not. My poor mother would find herself bombarded with random questions about my childhood and about our family amongst so many other topics, but she never hesitated to answer because she knew how much it all meant to me. Luckily, her excellent ability to remember details from nearly thirty years ago rarely failed her. I once asked why she really named me *Shufto*, a question I've asked many times before—more than any other. This was her response:

Question: "Mom, why did you really name me *Shufto*?"

Mom's answer: "I named you *Shufto* because, at the time of your birth, I didn't think I would be in the situation I was in with your father."

As a kid, I used to ask her about it so much I nearly drove her crazy. In the past her responses were always calm, collected, and she tried to reassure me it was a special name with a special meaning. For years, she resisted sharing her true feelings about it and never elaborated much on the matter until that moment. I was probably sixteen or seventeen years of age when we finally had this conversation. Prior to that, I had tried my best and did all I could to get Mom to reveal the full story. It was upsetting and frustrating to deal with, and I hated hearing the vague version of the story along with the inadequate answers she gave me. I guess she wanted to make sure I was old enough to understand the full story.

My mom is a strong woman, and she does not often mince words. She can be brutally honest, which she often is, but she's also very loving and purehearted. She may seem harsh and difficult to deal with from time to time, but it is nearly impossible to be upset with her or hold a grudge against her. When I turned sixteen, Mom started to speak with me more openly about certain topics. Suddenly, she was willing to elaborate on my father and his family and their history. I can tell these were sensitive topics for her, so I often took the time to listen instead of my usual approach of asking questions.

One day she explained the true meaning behind my name. She said, "*Shufto* is how I felt when things went wrong between your father and I, before, leading to, and after you were born. I felt I've seen it all, and that's why I named you *Shufto*. There was a heavy feeling deep in my heart, a feeling my situation could not possibly get any worse."

In *Cøllø (Shilluk)* culture, it is not unusual to name children after major events or occasions at the time of birth. Those names can often depend on the nature of the occasion. Children born during celebratory moments can be given specific names to remember and reflect on those happy times. Others born during times of mourning or sadness, such as after the loss of a loved one, may receive a different name to commemorate the family member. For instance, the name "*Mer*" means happiness or joy. The name "*Keem*" or "*Kimo*" is a common Cøllø name given to children born after the death of a relative, and the name "*Nyashanjwok*" (feminine) or "*Shanjwok*" (masculine) are typically given to children born on a Sunday. "*Shanjwok*" means Sunday, and my mom was born on a Sunday, so she was named *Nyashanjwok*.

There are many more common and uncommon names in *Cøllø* culture. Some are considered normal, others abnormal, and few are fully outrageous in their own right for reasons often only known to the mother, father, or both. However, my case was uniquely different, not necessarily due to the meaning behind it, but because *Shufto* is an Arabic word and not a *Cøllø/Shilluk* name.

Had my mother named me an *Cøllø* name, regardless of the meaning, it's possible my childhood experience could have been much different. The challenges I've faced as a result of the name *Shufto* could have been less traumatizing or entirely evaded. If my *Cøllø* name was just as unusual as *Shufto*, perhaps I could have learned to live with it a lot easier. The meaning behind a *Cøllø/Shilluk* name would have been limited to a select group of people who spoke and understood the language and its cultural significance. Opposite to the problem inherent in having an unusual Arabic name, which was understood by nearly everyone in Khartoum. The majority of the population speaks Arabic, and anyone who heard it immediately wondered if that was my real name or some sort of joke. As a kid, I was often asked the reason behind my name, who named me, and why would my mother name her son such an unheard-of name like *"Shufto?"* What could she have seen?

I felt like there was target painted on my back with big, bold red letters that read, "Take your best shot." With a name like Shufto, I quickly learned kids can be ruthless and extremely cruel. I was a walking, talking, and living joke, and it never ended. I constantly heard jokes like,*"Shufto shuno, ya Shufto?"* meaning, "What have you seen, Seen it?," Or, *"Shufto muno?"* meaning, "Who have you seen?" There were count-less other jokes I don't care to remember, and I hated hearing them as well. All of it made an already challenging childhood even more miserable, and I couldn't stand it. Unfortunately for my mother, she had to deal with the brunt of it because I gave her hell over it.

On my best days, I complained about the jokes I was subjected to on the regular bases by some of my friends and school mates. On my worst days, I was furious about the fact she chose such a name for me and asked to have my name changed immediately. I chewed her ear off often about changing my name to something normal like *Obej* or *Omojwok*, both *Cøllø* names I liked. I used to try my best to convince her to choose the name *Omojwok* because it means "God given" and I loved it. I thought if she did, it would solve my problem once and for all.

Needless to say, a name change was not in my immediate future, but my mother did try her best to make it up to me. One memorable example was my fourth birthday party. I can't imagine how she pulled it off, but my mom worked her magic to make it happen. She never talked about the sacrifices she made to have a birthday party at a time when only certain families could afford it. In our neighborhood alone, there were very few times a year when any of the kids attended a birthday party, let alone celebrated their own. I know my mom had to make a big sacrifice and probably had to use what little money she had saved up on my behalf.

Before I turned four years old, I never had a birthday party. That changed on March 8, 1993 when my mother surprised me with a party. There are a couple of reasons why it was so awesome. One, it was my first birthday party ever, which made it a huge deal. Two, the party was one of a few that year, along with two or three others in our neighborhood for kids with parents who were businessmen, worked for the government, or a non-governmental organization. Three, my mother made sure to make it an event worth remembering. She invited all my friends and other kids throughout the neighborhood, and they helped make it a celebration of a lifetime.

I vividly recall standing in the middle of all the kids with my birthday cake in front of me with four lit candles. My mother made so much *zalabia*(Sudanese fried dough), every kid at the party ate enough to their satisfaction. I was so happy about it because I loved eating *zalabia* as much as the next kid, and I still do. When it was time to blow out the candles, I took my sweet time blowing them out. After everyone finished singing, they waited a minute or two for me to make my wish and below out the candles.

I can still remember hearing the young and old voices singing the mixed Arabic-English version of the birthday song. *Happy birthday to you, happy birthday to you, happy birthday ya Shufto, happy birthday to you! Sana hilwa ya Jamel, Sana hilwa ya Jamel, Sana hilwa ya Jamel, Sana hilwa ya Jamel!.* The Arabic part roughly translates to *a beautiful year to you, handsome.*

After hearing the song, and as every voice in the background slowly faded into the distance, I took a deep breath and finally forced myself to blow out my four birthday candles. As everyone around me who gathered to celebrate my birthday started to clap and cheer, I felt nothing but pure joy in my heart. That was one of the first moments I felt my name wasn't a curse. It was just another name everyone around me, including the kids who usually tease me, and some of the adults who make rude and distasteful comments in attempt to be funny, were all there to celebrate. It felt amazing.

I was so happy and proud of my mom for the gift and joy she granted me that day. I consider that birthday celebration a reminder of one of the highlights of life in Khartoum. It was also the one and only birthday party I ever had in Sudan, but that never bothered me. I understood if my mom could have done it again, she would have. But unfortunately, life was quite difficult, and I knew some kids never had the opportunity to celebrate a single birthday the same way I did during my fourth birthday. For that, I am grateful and will always cherish and regard that day as one of the best days during my childhood in Khartoum, Sudan.

When I think about it, I'm reminded of the extent to which my mother has gone for me, and later on for my siblings and our family. There are so many other sacrifices she endured on my behalf when I was young, and that birthday memory often helps put them into perspective. Because of the type of woman she is, my mom would often go above and beyond not only for her children, but for her entire family. She would often set aside her own personal interests without hesitation for the people she loves and cares about.

As a child, I never noticed or realized how much my mom had sacrificed for me, nor did I have any idea she suffered for many years in silence for my sake. Since the very first day she held me in her arms, my mother has always done all she can to protect me from the harsh realities of life. I recall how she always steered clear from discussing certain topics with me growing up, particularly my father. When she finally decided it was okay to begin talking with me about him, she shared few details and tried to always paint him and his family in the best possible light. That's my mother, and that's who she's always been. As her oldest son, how can I not try my very best to be her little helper and always be there for her, when she has been there for me all my life.

I once asked my mother about her relationship with my father and his family. I asked if she could share more details than usual and elaborate on the nature of her relationship with the family, not my father. I was close to my aunt *Nyatow* and her family, my father's younger sister who lived in our neighborhood, but I did not know anyone else from the family very well. Like my father, they occasionally visited me when I was very young, and I only remember my grandmother, my dad's mom, visiting frequently.

I asked, "Mom, can you tell me about my dad's family? What were they like growing up?"

She responded and said, "Your dad's family are great people and they loved you very much." She continued, "Your uncles and aunts would always make it a point to come visit you whenever they were in town and made sure you were well. Your grandmother loved you most, and she regularly visited you and your cousins. She would insist I bring you to Omdurman to stay with her and the rest of the family for some time."

Listening to my mom talk about my dad's family always gave me conflicting feelings. How she felt toward my dad verses how she felt toward his family were quite different. However, she never shared them with me, at least not until I was much older. But I understood early on her feelings were complicated based on the little I had heard over the years.

My mother made it a point to never come across as vindictive or angry about anything that had to do with my dad, especially when it involved the rest of his family. At the same time, she spoke about the relationship she forged with the family on my behalf with genuine happiness. While she shared stories about those early days, I sometimes thought to myself, "How could the woman who named me *Shufto* because of my father be so loving toward his family?" The answer to that question would become more and more apparent the older I grew, and the more I discovered how truly amazing my mom is and always has been.

My father's family lived in the twin city of Omdurman, which lies on the western banks of the Nile across from the capital, Khartoum. It also happens to be a far distance from our neighborhood in Haj Yusef, which made it difficult to visit often. Luckily, because my aunt Nyatow and her family lived nearby in our neighborhood, I had direct contact with my dad's side of the family. She and my mother were as close as Cøllø customs permitted, given the complicated nature of her relationship with my father, but she loved me very much and treated me like her own child. I remember whenever I was allowed to go visit my aunt's house and spend time with her and my cousins, I felt at home and never out of place. My cousin *Shanjwok* (Bill) was older by approximately a year, and my cousin *Fajuan* was younger than me by approximately a year. If you didn't know we were cousins, you would have thought we were all brothers because we acted like it in every sense of the word.

Besides my aunt and her family, my grandmother was someone I was more familiar with as a child, but she passed away when I was young. I vaguely remember the days she visited; like any grandmother, she treated me with all kinds of special attention. She would bring treats with her, sit me on her lap, and smother me with all the affection in the world. I was very familiar with such behavior, which I often received from my other grandmother. My mom's mother had already conditioned me to expect the special grandchild treatment by that point. Still, there was something uniquely different about my dad's mother and the way she treated me. She never placed a hand or laid a finger on me for misbehaving. I remember that well because mom's mother lived with us and dad's mom did not. At home, my maternal grandmother was as tough when she needed to be as she was loving. However, my fraternal grandmother never needed to discipline me because she never witnessed me misbehaving and I loved it.

During those early years of my life, Mom told me she tried working things out with my dad and maintaining a healthy relationship with his family for my sake. Coming from a culture where family is central in every part of one's life, it was normal to rely on family members to help solve whatever issues couples faced especially when it involved children.

Mom told me, "When you were just barely a year old, (haboba) your grandma would insist I bring you to Omdurman and live with the family until your father and I worked things out. I would agree to take you and would stay for a month and sometimes longer with you to respect your grandma's wishes."

I asked once if she could tell me what that experience was like, and to my surprise she agreed to briefly talk about it.

She said, "I really enjoyed being with your dad's family, but the issue of his absence made things difficult. I understood his desire to pursue his education and become a doctor, and I was willing to be patient and wait for him even if it meant living with the family for much longer. But at the time, I did not see things improving between us, and there were other family matters that made it nearly impossible to see a way forward. I felt it was best for us to go back to my family."

I followed up with a few more questions in an attempt to extract more details. I asked, "What family issues stood in the way? Can you tell me what my father said about it?" I knew she wouldn't answer those pointed questions or elaborate on them, but I hoped she would reveal a little bit more details this time. I always respected that about Mom, and I never wanted to push her to the point of making these open and rare conversations toxic or unpleasant. They were special, a shared window to her past, our past, and a secret avenue to a life she once tried to build but could not build alone. They were glimpses of a family she wished to have, not only for her sake and happiness, but for me and my father as well.

CHAPTER 9

Young Rope Master

My first apprenticeship was working at a church across the street from our house. I was probably seven or eight years old when I gained interest in his work. At first, I spent a considerable amount of time watching him work on his unique craft, and then I grew curious about it and wanted to learn the craft myself. My teacher was an old man in his sixties, physically small in stature, and thin. He stood no more than five feet five inches tall and was soft spoken. He was basically the Sudanese version of Mr. Miyagi, the karate master played by Pat Morita from the classic film series The Karate Kid.[10] I was more or less his student, similar to the karate kid played by Daniel LaRusso in the original 1984 film.

I called him *Qay-yo or Qay-Qay,* which means grandfather in *Dhok Cøllø (Shilluk).* I called him that not because he was my grandpa, but out of respect. In *Cøllø* culture children do not address elders by name, instead by title such as grandpa, grandma, aunt, uncle, and so on. It's a common practice in most Sudanese communities, and ours was no different. Although he wasn't my grandpa per se, I later

---

10   Avildsen, *The Karate Kid, 1984.*

discovered he was in fact a relative. He was my grandmother's uncle, so the title "grandpa" turned out to be appropriate for addressing him.

Grandpa was a master at his craft; he weaved big, thick ropes from different articles of cloth. They were normally made of old bed sheets, window curtains, and other large articles of cloth. He had a unique way of weaving and turned these old items into ropes that looked braided like hair. They were always colorful and tough. I never asked where he got the endless supply of clothes, nor did I ask what those ropes were made for. I was just fascinated with the process of making what seemed like a collection of beautiful artwork.

My level of curiosity was through the roof. I wanted to learn about and do anything that slightly piqued my interest. Grandpa was gracious enough to foster my curiosity and let me watch him work and ask questions. He never dismissed me as some pesky little kid who was interfering with his work. Instead, he started to teach me about his unique rope craft. I would constantly ask him questions about the step-by-step process, and if he thought I was on the right course. I would often show him and compare my small version of his ropes and ask if it was the same quality. He would laugh and say, "Not yet, but it will be soon." I asked that question on day one of my apprenticeship, and every day after that.

After much practice, I eventually learned to perfect the basics of the rope-making process. First, I had to select and cut the right sheets down to size for smaller hands. Second, I had to properly learn how to wrap the cut sheets around my toes and hold them tight enough to weave and braid them tight. If I didn't, the rope would begin to unravel and it was a nightmare. I still had a long way to go before I could produce anything close to grandpa's quality, but I was determined to make progress over time. My ropes turned out much smaller and less colorful, but I was happy with my efforts and the skills I was learning to master.

I don't know exactly know how long the apprenticeship lasted since it's been so long, but probably for a few months during the summer break. I don't recall very well if I ever managed to make any quality ropes that were big and strong enough to be used for any real purpose, but I felt great knowing how to make one. I felt amazing about my capability to learn a new craft and working hard enough to master it to the best of my ability. Grandpa taught me more than just the art of rope making. He taught me the value of hard work and commitment in his own unique way. He taught me to take pride in what I choose to do, and to take the time needed to master it regardless of what it is.

It's an important lesson I took to heart and held on to ever since. Around the same time or shortly after, I became interested in my mother's traditional jewelry-making craft. She made beautiful traditional *Cøllø (Shilluk)* beaded necklaces and bracelets. The craft was becoming more popular at the time, and many other women and girls in our neighborhood were making other beaded items. They were in addition to the traditional *Cøllø* necklaces, bracelets, head, waste, and ankle beads already available. These custom items of jewelry were normally reserved for celebrations such as weddings and traditional gatherings. However, people were getting more creative and making new items such as key chains, rings, earrings, and so much more to sell. They sold them to foreigners, mostly missionaries or non-governmental organization personnel working in Sudan at that time.

My mother began shifting her focus from making the traditional beaded necklaces and bracelets to making more of the newly sought-after key chains and earrings. These items were becoming a more regular and a reliable source of income. I remember my mom telling me about this *Kawaja* (white woman) who bought from her and really liked the quality of her work. I had never met or seen the lady, but I knew she was mostly European or American and wanted to buy more of Mom's traditional jewelry. Mom also told me her favorite items where the beaded key chains.

The process of making jewelry and key chains was meticulous and time consuming. On average it took a few hours to complete making a single item because it was all done by hand, one bead at a time. You had to sit in the same place for hours threading a tiny string through a tiny colorful bead over and over until the job is done. It was difficult work, especially on the hands, eyes, and back, which I've also experienced firsthand trying to help. I knew Mom could only produce a few key chains per day not because she didn't want to make more, but due to the slow nature of the process of making these items. She also had to take care of us and attend to her other responsibilities throughout the household. She had to cook, clean, and take care of my younger siblings, which consumed much of her time during the day.

It was difficult watching Mom struggle to take care of all her household responsibilities, while trying at the same time to grow her jewelry business. She was essentially working two to three jobs at the same time and earning very little in return. Multitasking in Sudan wasn't as easy as one might imagine. First of all, cooking alone was a project that required my mom's full attention from beginning to end. Similar to many Sudanese households at the time, we did not have a stove and women cooked using man-made charcoal from burned wood called *fahaam*. My mother had to keep a close eye on the pot and make sure nothing burnt because *fahaam* can easily burn and constantly had to be monitored and adjusted to the right temperature. So, Mom had to either work early in the morning and start on one jewelry item, or during the day before she had to prepare dinner.

On occasion, she worked in the evenings right before sunset because there was no electricity in our neighborhood and oil lanterns and candles were often preserved mostly for emergency use. Some nights the moon was bright enough to help see without candles or lanterns, but it was still a challenge to avoid making mistakes. It was extremely difficult to differentiate between certain colors of tiny beads like white and yellow, or blue and black, under the moonlight, which wasn't exactly good for business.

Seeing how Mom was struggling to meet her quotas for keychains, bracelets, and the other jewelry items she had to meet, I felt the need to lend a helping hand. At first, I wasn't sure if I could be of any help, or if I would simply be a distraction. However, I decided to ask if she could teach me how to help make a key chain. It was a strange request because it was considered unusual for a boy, especially at my age, to take interest in such a craft. Traditionally, jewelry making was regarded as work for women and not men in *Cøllø* culture. I knew it was considered a women's job just like cooking and cleaning, but I didn't see it that way. My focus was on finding a way to help my mother, and learning this craft was one sure way to do so. Simply put, this was one more cool skill I could learn for a good reason, and Mom would be happy with me being her little helper.

Once my mom agreed to let me help by teaching me the basics of her craft, I was ready to learn and determined to do my best. I prided myself in being a fast learner and wanted to show I could manage to master the basics with relative ease. My first lesson was learning about the key chains Mom made, which were colorful and in the shape of crocodiles. I thought they were one of the coolest items in her portfolio, and I couldn't wait to learn how they were made so I could help add to it one crocodile at a time.

Mom made two types of crocodile key chains. One was considered the "basic croc" made with its mouth closed, or rather it didn't have an open mouth. The other I considered to be the "elaborate croc" made with its mouth open. The open mouth croc took more time and effort to make so it was more expensive. Naturally, I started to learn how to make the closed-mouth crocodile keychain first, and from what I can recall I learned it rather quickly. Within a few days, I made a quality product that passed my mother's rigorous inspection process. The open mouth croc took a little longer to learn because it's made from two parts combined in to one, which required some patience to perfect.

I became a reliable partner in my mom's small business and even managed to develop a little bit of a reputation around the neighborhood for my work. I was now, *Shufto, the boy who helps his mom with Teeg,*" (the *Cøllø* word for beads). I didn't mind the title; it was a good thing to be known around my neighborhood for something other than a smart mouth troublemaker with a strange name. It felt amazing helping Mom with her work, and all the hours we spent working together strengthened our mother-son relationship and we are better off for it.

CHAPTER 10

Goodbye, Khartoum

___

We left Khartoum, Sudan in early 1999 and immigrated to Cairo, Egypt. This was my first time leaving the country, and I did not know it was for good. The first part of our journey to Cairo consisted of a train ride thorough the dessert from Khartoum to Halfa, a city located on the northern Sudanese border with Egypt. I learned we were leaving Sudan not long before we left the country. My mother revealed the news a few weeks before it was time to depart from Khartoum.

Initially, I didn't know how to properly react because I did not have much time to process or think about what it all meant, but the idea of traveling to Cairo seemed like an adventure and I was excited about it. My mom, on the other hand, was a bit nervous but did well concealing it from my two younger siblings and me. I was preoccupied with my own preconceptions of what was to come on this once-in-a-lifetime adventure, and I didn't pay too much attention to her state of mind.

She was being strong for herself and for her three children. My two younger brothers Aken, Moum, and I were ages seven, five, and ten. My stepfather did not accompany us during this trip, but he was due to join us in Cairo in a matter of mouths. I didn't exactly know why he stayed behind, but I didn't ask. So, we said our goodbyes at the train terminal in Khartoum for the time being.

It was only a matter of hours after we departed from Khartoum before I started to feel bored and restless. We were in a train car with a number of other South Sudanese migrates traveling alongside us to Egypt. We shared our compartment with a *Cøllø* lady who was traveling alone to Cairo. My Mom struck a conversation with her, and they talked for hours during the long train ride. My two siblings were asleep for most of the trip, but I was not. While Mom and her new friend carried on with their conversation, I found myself staring out of the car window for hours on end. From the train off into the distance, the view seemed the same—a never-ending view of the Sudanese dessert.

The first hour or two after departing from Khartoum, there were glimpses of life in the dessert outside of the capital. I saw nomadic shepherds with livestock and men riding camel back. For the remainder of the trip, it seemed as if we were stuck in a time capsule in the middle of the dessert moving in an unknown direction and covering zero ground. Inside the train car, there was little to do in terms of fun. I was confined to our compartment and was not allowed to move around very much besides to go to the restroom. The seats in our section were old and not very comfortable, but they were spacious enough to fit Mom and all three of us. Overall, the train was old and took much longer to reach our destination.

We arrived in Halfa late the same day, and it was dark and possibly past midnight. I recall it wasn't very long before sunrise when Mom woke us and told us we had arrived. Shortly after we exited the train car, we walked a short distance and settled not far from lake Nubia. Mom left my brothers and me, along with our luggage, outside the train station with her new friend that had been traveling alongside us from Khartoum. A short time later, Mom retuned with food for all of us. It was freshly prepared fried fish with bread, and my brothers and I were half asleep eating the food before dozing off for a few more hours. We did not have any accommodation for the night, prearranged or otherwise, and Mom probably did not have enough money in her budget to book a room for as at the local inn. We waited at the same location outside for hours that morning until it was time to board the boat for Aswan.

As we made our way to board the vessel, I couldn't help but notice some stark difference between Halfa and Khartoum. The people in Halfa seem gentler and easier going compared to those living in Khartoum. There was a gentle breeze in the air that felt pleasant and reminded me of early mornings in Shigla during Christmas days. It felt like a breath of fresh air, cool and gentle just like December mornings in Khartoum, but slightly different. When we finally arrived near the dock in preparation to board the ferry, that's when it all started to make sense. I looked out in Lake Nubia, a sight like nothing I have ever seen before, and it was amazing. When I felt the breeze from this massive body of water up close and personal, I started to understand why someone can feel so much more relaxed living in Halfa instead of in Khartoum.

From Halfa to Aswan was roughly one day's journey through the waters of lake Nubia into Lake Nasser in Southern Egypt. Aswan is Egypt's southernmost city located at the east bank of the Nile River. The city is known for its diverse and rich history and culture through Egypt. The food in Aswan was among the best I'd ever tasted outside of Sudan, and the majority of its residences shared close physical resemblance to North Sudanese. They were noticeably darker in complexion then their northern countrymen in Cairo, Alexandria, and other regions in Egypt, and they were also more accommodating.

The city had a lovely view of the River Nile, especially at night when the city lights were on full display. The bright lights were the first thing I set my sights on from miles away as we approach the docks. The view from aboard the vessel was like nothing I'd ever seen before and it was mesmerizing. There were restaurants and shops overlooking the riverbanks, fully lit and bustling with people. There was the sound of Egyptian music coming from all sides, and small boats anchored on both backs of the river as we slowly passed by, inching closer toward our final destination. I was amazed, filled with excitement, and recall thinking, *Wow, I can't believe we're finally in Egypt.*

CHAPTER 11

EGYPT

———

Aswan was a wonderful first glimpse of Egypt and, despite being there for less than a day, I felt good about how our transition was going so far. As we made our way through the city to the train station, I was fascinated by the Egyptian-Arabic dialect I was hearing all around me. Hearing Egyptian accents for the first time in person was quite interesting even though I was already familiar with it. I've watched many Egyptian movies and television series in Khartoum, but none quite sounded the same as hearing it in real life.

When we first arrived in Cairo, we lived with relatives for the first few months. My uncle *Tuwoal* and his family hosted us in his home along with a few other relatives. He had been living in Cairo with his family for a number of years before our arrival and had managed to do quite well for himself professionally. He was an associate pastor at a community church located in *Maadi*, one of Cairo's high-end neighborhoods. Just a few months before our arrival, there were other relatives who made it to Egypt, including two of my uncles who were both in their early twenties and lived with us temporarily. It was a full house for the first few months until we were able to fully transition into our new life on our own in Cairo.

My uncle *Tuwoal* and his family welcomed us with open arms into their luxurious three-bedroom apartment in the heart of *Maadi*. The apartment was essentially a penthouse on the top floor of a seven-story apartment building. It had three large bedrooms, two massive living rooms, a kitchen, a bathroom, and my personal favorite, a huge decorative outdoor space. The apartment was beautiful like nothing I've ever seen or lived in, or even stepped a foot into, before in Sudan. The balcony was massive and had an amazing view overseeing the beautiful night skyline of one of Cairo's best neighborhoods. I spent a good amount of my free time hanging out there with my siblings and little cousins.

For a ten-year-old Sudanese kid born and raised in an impoverished and underdeveloped neighborhood in Khartoum, the sight alone from the top of an apartment building was breathtaking. I recall spending many nights outside on the balcony staring at the apartment buildings surrounding our own all lit up. On those nights, I often wondered how Egyptians managed to build such tall structures. I had little to compare this new experience to, and the closest structures I saw in Sudan that were remotely close to Egypt, were five-to-six-story buildings still under construction in Khartoum. The only other fully developed buildings I saw were owned by either the government or financial institutions.

We lived with my uncle and his family in Maadi for about three months. My stepfather was still in Khartoum during that time period, and we moved out when he finally arrived in Cairo. We waited for him because it would have been difficult for my Mom and her three sons to venture out on our own. My two younger brothers Aken and Moum were approximately ages six and four, and I was ten years old. Had my siblings and I been older, or if I was old enough to work and help support the family, my mother might have been more comfortable moving without my stepdad. We could have managed to go out on our own in a city like Cairo without the support from a second parent.

My uncle and his family were extremely gracious for allowing us to live with them for those three months. It was typical for new families and individuals to live with relatives for a month or two when they first arrived in Egypt, but not for three months or more. Not only was it unusual, but it also often led to tension and rifts between family members. Fortunately for us the positives outweighed the negatives, and those months even gave us a chance to begin laying the groundwork for the next chapter of our lives.

Prior to my stepdad's arrival, my mom started the process of applying for asylum through the UNACAF refugee resettlement program. Many families and individuals typically started the application process within the first few months of their arrival, and Mom did so during our second or third month in Cairo. Initially, she had appointments and meetings with the program's case workers and individuals responsible for screening applicants. During that first step my uncle Timothy, one of the young men living with us at the time, offered to help her navigate through the process and connect with the right people for additional help. He helped make sure the application for resettlement was properly completed and connected Mom with Arabic to English translators, which was crucial to ensure none of the important steps were missed.

As the process went on, Uncle Timothy was not able to continue to help in the same capacity nor was there anyone else in my uncle's house available to take his place. All the adults were busy working or trying to navigate through their own application processes. All of the sudden, Mom was in a difficult position because she could not afford to withdraw her application because there was no telling what might happen after the fact. She didn't know if it was possible to pause the process until she could find further assistance, or if it was possible to initiate a new process after my stepdad made it to Egypt in a matter of months.

Seeing my mother under so much distress made me feel the need to do something. I didn't know what exactly I could do to help, but I couldn't simply sit around and watch her continue to struggle. I had already figured out how to navigate Cairo's transit system by that time. The "metro," as it was commonly referred to in Egypt, had three lines crisscrossing throughout the city. The first line was above ground, and I quickly became very familiar with it while running errands for the family, but the second and third lines not so much. Luckily, the first line was all I needed to know about to help guide Mom to and from the refugee resettlement offices. In addition, my ability to speak Egyptian Arabic was improving rapidly, so I was confident enough to serve as a semi-translator for Mom when needed.

I was ten going on eleven years old when I started helping Mom through our "UN" process, as it was commonly known. On many occasions, I had to go pick up or drop off documents at the UN office by myself because Mom had to stay home with the kids or wasn't feeling well. Those days became more frequent as the weeks went on. We discovered she was pregnant and nearing her third trimester. This was something we didn't know prior to leaving Khartoum roughly seven months earlier, as her due date inched closer. However, nothing about that situation felt abnormal, and I felt my duty was to simply be there to help as much as possible. After all, I was the oldest child in my family as well as in my uncle's household.

On an average day I was asked to run multiple errands for almost every adult in the apartment and ran up and down the fourteen or so sets of stairs to reach our seventh-floor apartment. I didn't mind it, but there was a point when my mother became angry about it because she thought the routine was getting out of control, especially when I was asked to go out late in the evenings or at night. On the other hand, I became very familiar with a good portion of the city of Cairo and learned a lot about the way of life in Egypt within a few short months. Back then, it was quite normal for a kid my age to go across town and back home in one piece. I'm thankful for that because things changed drastically just a few years after that.

ABASEYA—NEW NEIGHBORHOOD

Approximately three months after the family migrated to Egypt, my stepdad Natale arrived from Khartoum. He stayed behind to continue working and earn enough money for a ticket to Cairo. At the time, it wasn't unusual for Sudanese families to separate for a period of time in hopes of reuniting once again later on. Of course, reunification wasn't always guaranteed. For families like ours leaving Khartoum for Cairo, it was common for mothers and young children to first migrate to Egypt. Fathers along with older children would often reunite with the rest of the family in a few months. However, it was sometimes a matter of years, and unfortunately for some families, the opportunity to reunite never presented itself.

My family was amongst the luckier ones. We had relatives who were well established in Egypt, and they were able to host us for months before my stepdad arrived. There were many other Sudanese families who were not so lucky and did not have anyone to support them in Egypt. No one hosted them temporarily, and no one helped with the transition to a new society quite different from what they were used to in Sudan. The transition process was not easy for most, and I can only imagine how much more difficult it would have been without assistance from family or friends.

About a month or so after my stepfather made it to Cairo in the spring of 1999, we moved out of my uncle's place and into a small two-bedroom apartment across town. We moved to the neighborhood of *Abaseya*, which was very different from what we've grown used to in the upscale neighborhood of *Maadi*. *Abaseya* was one of the poorer parts of the city with noticeably older buildings, narrower streets, and was quite congested. It was very much the opposite of everything in *Maadi*, including the price tag for an apartment.

We moved into a first-floor apartment located just minutes away from the main road, in a part of the neighborhood that felt most familiar to Sudanese living in Cairo. This was both good and bad depending on one's perspective. It was good because of the proximity to the main church and school most Sudanese attended. It was bad because of the foot traffic and high frequency of random and unannounced visits from other Sudanese in the area. In addition, we were not the only occupants in this small, narrow, two-bedroom apartment; we had to share with another family.

They were a family of four, a husband and wife with a young daughter and their niece. The husband was close with my stepdad and they were longtime friends from Sudan. They were also new to Cairo and arrived in Egypt around the same time as my stepfather. Our family was slightly larger with a total of five people, my Mom, stepdad, my two brothers, and myself. Not very long after we moved in, we welcomed our newest member of the family, a baby girl by the name of Adut. She is the first and only one of my siblings born in Egypt and was the youngest and only girl in the family at the time.

When we moved in, the apartment was refurnished, which was typical in Cairo. Anyone can rent a super luxury massive apartment with a rooftop view just like my uncle's apartment, or a three hundred square foot New York City style studio, depending on your budget. You can find a place in *Maadi* or in other areas of the city that were nicer and quiet, or in a questionable part of town an hour's walk from the Metro station. The closer you were to the nicer neighborhoods and to the main Metro lines and bus routes, the more expensive the rent.

Our apartment was closer to the New York City studio description, but not quite as expensive. The two bedrooms were each furnished with bedding and one old antique dresser. The living room had a sofa that also doubled as a bed. It had a worn-out red cloth over it that looked like an old curtain, and it was hard as a rock for some reason. The sofa was placed against the wall directly across from the front door and did not recline, adjust, and was difficult to move from that location. There were also some antique chairs placed across from the television set inches away from the front door. The old TV set took up a good portion of the space between the door on the left side and the hallway on the right. We had to be very careful opening and closing the door so as to not damage the TV.

The kitchen and bathroom were pretty small and similar in size, and both were located toward the back of the apartment. The kitchen was just a few feet past the TV set and the sofa, with a small stove and refrigerator inside. Both were old but functional, just like everything else in the apartment. The kitchen space itself was big enough to fit one adult at a time, and the rest of the space was taken up by kitchen cabinets and the sink. The bathroom was smaller, about half the size of the kitchen, with no bathtub or standup shower. It had a shower drain on one corner and a sink and toilet at another. Both were designed and built in a way that left approximately three feet or so for the hallway connecting the rest of the apartment.

My family occupied the smaller bedroom next to the front door and across from the TV set. The room was probably about sixty square feet in size and only had one window that opened out into the noisy street. The bed in the room was no bigger than a single or double mattress, and there was barely room for anything else, not even a sleeping bag. The second bedroom was bigger with a larger bed, perhaps a full-size or even a queen mattress. I'm not sure how my family ended up with the smaller bedroom given there were more of us, but we did. At first it was no big deal with just the five of us but with the birth of my baby sister, it became more difficult for my parents to manage in the smaller space.

My mom and stepfather occupied the room and stored most of our belongs with them, and my two younger brothers and I were out in the living room. The second family all slept in the other bedroom, which was large enough to accommodate all four of them. During the day, the living room was shared and available to everyone, including our frequent guests, but at night it was a bedroom for my brothers and me. That was the arrangement for the few first months, until we had two more people join the household for the duration of our time in Cairo.

Our new roommates were newcomers to Egypt and were relatives of the other family. They were a young couple in their mid-to-late twenties. The boyfriend was the younger brother of my stepdad's friend, but I hadn't met the girlfriend before moving in with us. It was understandable why they needed to live with us temporarily, similar to our experience at my uncle's when we first arrived in Egypt. It was customary to welcome family or friends, and to host for a while until they are acquainted with life in Egypt. However, our living conditions were not ideal for that situation and the already jam-packed unit we lived in made things more difficult and complex. For the new couple, living with us meant having to share the small living space with my two young brothers and me. It was obviously less than ideal not only for us, but for them as well. Frankly, it was pretty uncomfortable having to share such a small space with two grown adults. However, there was certainly nothing I could say or do about it. My little brothers and I had to simply manage and see what happened next.

LIFE IN CAIRO

Despite the overcrowded situation in our small apartment, living in *Abaseya* could be described as an upgrade compared to life in *Shigla, Haj Yousif.* How big of an upgrade? That depends on who you ask and their experience in Egypt. For some people, it was a decent or pleasant year or two. Those were the families and individuals who went through the refugee resettlement process without or with very few issues, like my family. For others, it was a challenging three to five years, perhaps because they faced some issues or were denied asylum once or twice, or because there were facing other setbacks during those years. For most Sudanese refugees, life in

Egypt became their new normal with no way out. Those were the people who claimed asylum, but were denied resettlement on multiple occasions and simply decided to stay put and make do with what they had available to them.

As an eleven-year-old kid, I didn't think about those issues because they never crossed my mind. I was preoccupied with what life in Cairo had to offer compared to Khartoum. At first, I thought the availability and access to basic utilities such as running water, indoor plumbing, electricity, and paved roads were major upgrades from what I was accustomed to in Sudan. Access to regularly available public transportation through numerous bus routes and the metro were day and night compared to Sudan. We didn't have the infrastructure nor the resources to invest in such public goods, and so it was interesting to see the differences it made in the lives of average citizens.

In Khartoum, none of those services were available to the overwhelming majority of the population. Even fewer of those services stretched close to the neighborhoods occupied by majority of South Sudanese living in the capital. In *Shigla, Haj Yousif* where I was born, there was no electricity or running water. I remember having to walk everywhere because everything was within "walking distance," and during the rare occasions when we left the neighborhood, we walked quite a distance to the bus station. There, private microbuses were available for hire and served as "public" means of transportation, or *mosallot* in Arabic. The informal bus station was also where the paved road ended, which was at the edge of our neighborhood. It was at least a twenty- to thirty-minute walk under the hot sun, and always felt like a road trip to a place I've never been. In Egypt, that feeling faded away almost instantly because of the increased availability of such basic necessities. It provided a certain feeling of appreciation for life in Cairo.

It's hard to believe we lived in Egypt for just about a year because of all we experienced during that time. I consider my family to be among the fortunate groups of people who migrated to Egypt, applied for resettlement, and were accepted within that time frame. Our entire application process roughly lasted about the same time we spent living in Cairo. For a select number of Sudanese refugees who upended their lives back home, left everyone and everything they knew behind, it turned out to be the best possible scenario. Many people took the risk and migrated to Egypt in hopes of finding a better life, but not all were fortunate enough to have been accepted into the resettlement program.

The fourteen months or so we spent in Cairo were quite intense, and my family and I experienced many ups and downs. That period was a time filled with uncertainty, hardship, and rapid change for all of us with glimmers of light at the end of the tunnel. Ultimately, it was a very difficult time, particularly for my parents. There were a number of factors that made life so difficult. To cover the cost of housing, my stepdad had to work twelve-hour shifts six to seven days a week at a factory. He earned approximately three hundred Egyptian pounds a month, the equivalent of earning roughly $88.00 a month USD, $22.00 a week, or $0.30 an hour for a seventy-two-hour work week.

The wages he earned were barely enough to cover the cost of rent alone, so there was a desperate need for additional income in our family. This meant my mother had to join the work force to supplement our household income and cover the cost of food and other necessities. Mom was still caring for our newborn sister Adut at the time, but the family was pressed for income. Under normal circumstances, Mom would have had enough time to nurse the baby until she was at least six months before thinking about going back to work. However, we were no longer in Sudan where that may have been possible. Instead, we were now living in Egypt, a much more demanding country.

My mother was no stranger to hard work, and in fact she had been "hustling" for a long time to take care of us. Throughout my childhood in Sudan, I'd known Mom to have been working at least a few different jobs at any given time. In Cairo, things were very different with less favorable conditions to make ends meet. For instance, in Sudan childcare was no issue. Living with my grandparents meant there were relatives around who could help look after the children. I had so many aunts and uncles around me growing up that it was nearly impossible to go unseen for more than ten minutes. It also meant you couldn't get away with anything because one of them was always around with a belt or *mufraka* (Sudanese wooden kitchen utensil) nearby.

Needless to say, I did not miss the strict disciplinary protocol I was often subjected to, but I did miss the family structure we had which would've been helpful in Egypt. I missed it mostly for my Mom because I realized how much of a support system it was for her. Without support, my mother had to figure out a way to find childcare and go find work as a housekeeper in some Egyptian's household. Housekeeping was one of the few available jobs for Sudanese and other immigrant and refugee women in Egypt.

Fortunately for us, there was a Sudanese family that moved into the apartment adjacent to ours. They were a big family with many children across the age spectrum. Some were younger, other were around my age, and two were older teenagers. For Mom, this was a blessing because their parents were in a similar situation and understood my family's predicament. They had to both work and relied on their teenage children to watch over their younger siblings. Mom asked them if it would be okay for one of their teenage kids to keep an eye on my siblings and me, and thankfully they agreed.

The couple instructed their oldest daughter to check in on my siblings and me across the hall at least a few times a day. After a week or two, we started going over to their apartment for a good portion of the day. This arrangement allowed my mother to start working knowing her young daughter and three boys were not home alone all day. Instead, she could breathe a bit easier knowing they were looked after by a responsible young lady.

MOM'S FIRST AND LAST JOB IN CAIRO

When my mom started working, my responsibilities as the oldest child in the household intensified. She started working for an Egyptian family as a housekeeper earning about twenty-five Egyptian pounds per day. This was the equivalent of earning $7.36 a day working forty to fifty hours a week. Every day as I watched my mother and stepfather leave for work, I had to start thinking about my new responsibilities as the eldest, which was to watch over and care for my baby sister, my two brothers, and the daughter and niece of the other family in our household.

Initially, I did not realize how much pressure was being placed on my shoulders nor was I able to fully comprehend it at the time. Maybe that was a good thing because at that age I could have easily been overwhelmed. Thankfully I was able to quickly develop a routine that was pretty consistent and worked well. In the morning an hour or so after my mother left to catch the early bus for work, I would start preparing my two brothers for school and walk them down to class. I escorted them, along with the two young girls living with us, to the church where they attended morning classes. I would then come back home to watch and care for my baby sister until the boys were out of school in the afternoon around 2:30–3:00 p.m. I then went back to the school to pick them up, and once back home, I made sure everyone had dinner before preparing myself for school in the evening.

Five days a week this was essentially my daily routine except during the holidays. Fortunately, the schoolhouse was located at a Catholic church on the main road just minutes from our apartment building. This meant my commute in the morning with the kids was about ten minutes and it was roughly about the same going back home with them in the afternoon. In the evenings however, I always rushed back and forth to make sure I was not late for school or to get back home.

Living so close to *Sakakini* was a blessing for many reasons, but for one in particular. *Sakakini* was, and still is, one of the best-known Catholic churches in Cairo to Sudanese. The official name of the church is Scared Heart Roman Catholic Church, but it is commonly known as *Sakakini*, which is the name of the road it is located on. Over the years the church has gained notoriety and a repetition for being the ultimate gathering place for South Sudanese in Cairo. Most of them attended Sunday mass at the church, but during the rest of the week the church was also full of people gathered for many other reasons.

The church became one of the only places in Cairo where you can find just about anyone. People new in Cairo often met friends and relatives in *Sakakini* they didn't know were in Egypt, and they sometimes ran into others they had lost contact with since leaving Sudan. It was common practice to ask around and gather information from regulars who spent much of their time at the church, and more than likely they were able to help. Whilst we were in Cairo, almost all events and gatherings we attended were held at *Sakakini*. The majority of them were weddings and celebrations that attracted many people.

I always looked forward to my time at the church, whether it was for Sunday mass, my routine evening classes, or large celebratory events. I was excited about it because it was an opportunity to breakout of the cycle and be myself, be a regular eleven-year-old kid and do what eleven-year-old kids normally did. I wanted nothing more than to be around other kids my age, make friends, and have a good time playing around and laughing at silly things. That was my idea of normalcy in Egypt, which was very different compared to Sudan. At school during the evenings was the closest I felt to being a typical eleven-year-old kid because being in class with my new friends felt amazing and I loved it.

.

CHAPTER 12

Mom's Accident

One of the most horrific and difficult times we faced in Egypt was my mother's accident. She and I had a conversation recently about that particular time in Egypt. She recalled how the accident happened and how I took it upon myself to find a way to help. The accident happened one evening when Mom was on her way home from work. The story goes, as she was stepping off the bus, the driver decided to pull off before she had fully and safely stepped off the bus, causing her to fall off. When that happened, she fell onto her left side and broke her left arm.

The bus driver did not stop to check on her or at all; he drove off as if nothing unusual had just occurred. Mom said she remembered thinking the act was intentionally meant to harm her and the driver knew exactly what he was doing. She was shocked someone would commit such an act against a stranger for no apparent reason. Thankfully, there were a few good Samaritans nearby who came to her aid and took her to the hospital for treatment. During that conversation, my mom asked me, *"Inta maszakir?"* meaning "Do you remember? When you went to ask for help from the church you occasionally went to with the Lebanese priest?" My responded was, "I did?"

I remember there were about three or four catholic churches I was familiar with but spent most of my time at *Sakakini* where I attended school and Sunday mass. The other churches had programs on different days of the week that provided assistance to the Sudanese population in Cairo. Life was extremely difficult for most families, mine included, and we sought out assistance wherever available. Churches provided the most support, and I was essentially the letter carrier for the family. Whatever it was, whether a message or a package, I was available for pick-up or delivery free of charge.

My frequent visits to the different churches provided an opportunity to meet many of the clergy, staff, and volunteers. I also met many in the congregation who regularly attended the church, and I became a familiar face. Every time my mother asked me to go somewhere or to see someone, I made it a point to execute that task exactly as instructed so I could be back as soon as possible just in case she needed me for something else. I was already very protective of my mom, but after the accident I was now also afraid for her. I didn't want to be far away from her, and I didn't want to be absent when she needed me, and I certainly didn't want her to feel helpless or alone. I wanted her to know she could rely on me, always.

During those months when Mom was still recovering from the accident, I was in and out of the apartment more frequently running light errands. Since she was no longer working, I didn't have to spend most days at home with my siblings anymore. I still had most of my routine in place, but I now had time to go out more not only for my Mom, but for my neighbors, and even for our Egyptian landlord. Apparently, I developed somewhat of reputation for being a reliable kid who could be sent out to run light errands when our neighbors and landlord got wind of it.

Our landlord was an interesting character. His name was Said but we called him *Ammo* (fraternal uncle) Said. He was a very nice old man, and he very much reminded me of my grandfather. He lived on the seventh or eighth floor of the building with his wife, and they both had a little bit of trouble climbing up and down all those flights of stairs. He had adult children who lived on different floors of the same building, but I rarely saw them. I knew one of his sons was a police officer but didn't know much about the rest of their families. *Ammo* Said occasionally needed help with light errands, and so I offered to help as much as I can.

I went out to buy groceries for my family on a daily basis, so I didn't mind adding a few extra things on my list for *Ammo* Said on occasion. It was the right thing to do, and I figure it would be good to help out the old man with a few errands. Every time I went out, I started to check if he and his wife needed anything from the store, and I regularly offered to pick up whatever they needed on my way back home. I didn't need to walk up seven or eight flights of stairs to ask if they needed anything, instead they shouted out their shopping list from the balcony and lowered the money with a basket attached to a long rope. It was normal and a regular part of life in Egypt to hear people shouting up and down an apartment building or anywhere really, so it became our usual means of communication. They also spent a good amount of time on their balcony, so it worked perfectly.

Mom once told me about a story *Ammo* Said shared with her about one of our rare ventures together to the local shop. He and I occasionally when to the store together, and that's usually when he needed to get out of the building for a while. He told my mom about what happened that particular day, which I honestly didn't quite remember as well as she described it. This happened sometime after we were accepted for resettlement to the United States. While making small talk with the store clerk, he broke the news and told the clerk my family was preparing to leave the country for America in a few short months. The clerk turns to me and asked, "Have you taken your picture yet?" I answered, "Yes." He then asked, "So what did the picture come out to look like?" I answered, "Like me."

At that exact moment, *Ammo* Said started laughing out loud because he knew the clerk was trying to make a joke in a typical Egyptian fashion—often filled with sarcasms, disrespect, and insults all wrapped up in one and disguised as a joke. By asking such a question, the clerk was looking to make a joke about my dark skin complexion and was implying my picture must have come out too dark because of the melanin. Instead, I turned the tables, and the joke was on him, something I learned to do quite well when dealing with characters like him. According to Mom, I didn't laugh about it, but *Ammo* Said was having the time of his life. He was laughing at the clerk, who seemed stunned until the very moment we walk away, leaving him behind still in awe of my smart mouth.

When we got back home, *Ammo* Said explained to my mom what just happened. He was still chuckling about it and told her in Arabic, "Your son is something else. He knew the clerk was trying to make a joke about his picture coming out too dark because of his complexion, but instead he made the shopkeeper look pretty stupid about it. I'm going to miss him very much. *Allah ma-ak*," meaning "God be with you."

A few days later is when I went to the church to ask for help on behalf of my Mom and explained to the Lebanese priest she recently was involved in an accident. I told the priest she suffered a broken arm and would not be able to work for a while. My mother recalled I came back home from the church and explained to her the priest had suggested she come back with me. He instructed I go home and ask my mother to accompany me back to the church so he could see if she indeed had been in an accident.

His instructions were a bit unusual, but I didn't think anything of it. I simply felt to secure help for Mom, I had to obey the words of the priest. So, I agreed and promised to go straight home then bring my mother back with me to the church. That's exactly what I did. I went straight home and asked my mother to accompany me back to the church as promised for proof of her injury.

Mom explained, "You came home and said to me the priest asked to bring me back with you to the church, to see if what you told him about my accident was true. We then managed to make our way to the church through the busy public transportation system, and you carried your infant baby sister. With my one arm in a cast, all I could do was watch you and your sister while you carried her all the way to the church." I remember exactly how packed the public transportation system always was in Cairo, especially on some of the main routes. Unfortunately for us, those routes were the closest to our apartment, and we regularly had to use them. I can only imagine the level of anxiety my mother felt watching her eleven-year-old son carry her infant daughter through a crowd of people while trying to protect her broken arm.

Once we reached the church, Mom recalled the priest was surprised I managed to actually come back with her as promised. I guess he must have thought I was making up this crazy and tragic story just to get one over on him. I can't imagine what I may have said or done to make him doubt or question me. It didn't matter; I was more concerned with the church being able to help my mother. I don't recall what they talked about, but Mom later told me the priest was so surprised a kid my age would take the initiative and go through all that trouble to try finding help for his family. On the same day, Mom said the priest briefly left and came back with a bag full of household items. He gave us a large bag filled with soap, canned goods, bread, and a bunch of other things. He also presented my mother with a cash gift of one hundred forty Egyptian pounds, a substantially large cash donation at the time.

UN ACCEPTANCE

When we received our acceptance letter for resettlement to America, people regularly asked my mother, "Where are you going to be moving to aboard?" The answer was "New York." Not long after the announcement, my mother made me her spokesperson. I was very comfortable shouting out "New York" and happy to affirm her answer every time someone asked. I did so with my best imitation of an American accent. For a couple of months before our scheduled travel date, it became routine to share that answer with everyone who asked. Before we landed at John F. Kennedy International Airport (JFK), and then the Buffalo-Niagara International Airport in western New York, I did not know New York was also a state. Before then, we all were under the impression New York only meant New York City. Once we arrived in Buffalo, I then discovered the existence of New York State, the empire state, one of fifty states with many cities, towns,

and villages, including one of the world's largest metropol-
itans—the Big Apple.

According to my Mom, we almost didn't make the list of
families relocating out of Egypt. On the day we were confirmed to have been accepted for resettlement, my mother
reminded me of a major issue that almost prevented us from
leaving Egypt. During our appointment, the case manager
stipulated we must present our headshot photos the same day,
or else we would no longer be eligible to continue our process
for resettlement. I told my Mom I honestly didn't remember,
but she continued to explain what happened in hopes of trig-
gering my memory. She thought that was it, our opportunity
to migrate out of Egypt was slipping through her fingers,
and she didn't know what to do. She asked me, "*Muzakkar?*"
meaning, "Remember?" She continued, "Remember the
moment when you suggested we go see your uncle and ask
for help because your stepdad and I did not have the money
needed to take the photos required for our case?"

I said in response, "I'm honestly struggling to remember
that day, but I'll try my best." Mom responded and said "We
needed forty Egyptian pounds to pay for the pictures. They
requested photos for your stepdad and me, you, your two
brothers, and your infant sister who was barley six months
old at the time. Your stepdad and I racked our brains trying
to figure out what do, and that's when you suggested taking
the metro to *Maadi* because they didn't charge children for
metro fees, to ask your uncle for help."

I still couldn't piece together the details of that day the
same way my mother remembers, but I knew it must have
happened the way she described it. One, my mother has the
best memory out of anyone I know and never seems to forget
many details, also she was right about the fact kids rode the

metro free of charge. I used to ride the metro often and ran across town regularly for less pressing matters. This was very important and I would've done whatever needed without hesitation. Mom finally concluded by saying, "Luckily that day your uncle was home which was surprising because he usually kept a busy schedule especially during the day. He was able to help by loaning us the forty pounds required to cover the cost of those photos we needed to go to America."

Apparently, had things turned out differently without help from my uncle, my family would have not been able to board the flight to America. It is very likely we wouldn't have eventually made to Buffalo, New York on that beautiful spring evening on April 28, 2000. I can't imagine what life may have tuned out like for my family and me had we remained in Egypt all these years. I'm certain it would have been very much different than what it is now. The reality is, similar to most refugee families and individuals around the world, my family and I would have been in no position for me to share my story as I am now.

CHAPTER 13

United States of America

My family and I arrived in Buffalo, New York on Friday, April 28, 2000. Twenty-four hours before, we were preparing to leave one country for yet another country we knew next to nothing about. Unlike Egypt, an Arabic-speaking country that shares a border with my country of birth, America was a completely different world. We spent most of the day packing clothes and giving away things we couldn't take with us to family and friends who were visiting to see us off and say their goodbyes. During these last hours in Cairo, it was customary to welcome visitors to your home for hot tea and for what can only be described best as a sort of story time for adults.

The topic of conversation was normally dominated by unsolicited advice about life in America, Australia, or Canada based on hearsay. That evening was no different. Between the sounds of laughter coming from the living room where the adults gather, you could hear a bit of sadness from my Mom and her friends' voices. That was a reality check and a reminder the time to part ways was fast approaching, and there was no telling if they would ever see each other again or if it was time to say goodbye forever.

On our way to the airport that evening, there were a handful of close relatives and friends who accompanied us. It was an emotional departure for everyone, particularly my Mom, but it was also full of excitement. This was officially the first time any of us had ever stepped foot in an airport, and I had been looking forward to it. I remember going through security and the boarding process at Cairo International Airport for the first time, and it was quite different back then compared to now. Nonetheless, I was fascinated by everything around me at the airport, the high-end stores, the many pilots and flight attendants rushing past us, and the diverse groups of people all over the airport. I wasn't used to seeing so many non-Egyptians or Sudanese all in place.

When we finally boarded the plane, that is when it truly hit home. First, I was shocked and surprised by how massive the aircraft was, and second, I couldn't believe the large number of passengers aboard it. I genuinely did not expect to see so many people on anything other than a passenger ship or a train. But there was no time to stand around wondering and trying to figure out how a plane of that size was able to fly with so many people. I had to follow my parents to our seats and luckily for me, I was assigned a window seat.

I can recall with absolute clarity, the moment we took off the runway more than any else for one simple reason: the view over Cairo from the airplane's window. For the first time ever, I was looking out over an entire city from a plane, and it was an amazing sight to see. I was reminded of the first time I saw the night sky of Aswan from aboard the ferry that carried us from Wadi Halfa in Sudan. This time however, the view was quite different in every sense of the word and it was amazing.

It was now official: my family and I were off to America, from Egypt, across the African continent, over the waters of the Atlantic Ocean, and into North America. Now all there was left to do was wait until it was time to land in New York. That proved to be easier said than done within the first few hours in the air. I was wide awake and my mind was running wild trying to imagine what was in store for us across the ocean. Thank God for inflight entertainment.

During the flight I ended up spending much of my time watching movies. My excitement for all that was happening kept me from sleeping, and I just couldn't wait to touch down on American soil. It also didn't help other passengers seemed to be constantly moving around the cabin. Every few minutes someone was going up or down the aisles to the restroom or walking around to stretch their legs. There were moments I managed to doze off for a little while but ended up disturbed by the slightest sounds. After that happened a few times I decided to make the best of the remaining flight time by watching more movies and listening to music.

When we finally landed at JFK, first I was relieved we had landed safely. Second, I was relieved my family and I were that much closer to reaching our destination and our new home. Initially I thought finally we're in New York, a place we've been talking about for years and only dreamed of visiting one day. The "Big Apple" is a city known to so many people around the world and can be easily recognized through its many landmarks and symbols. There would be the Statue of Liberty, the World Trade Center or the Twin Towers, and numerous other iconic structures throughout the city. It all seemed surreal and I knew it was going to take some time to get used to this new reality and everything that was happening at the time.

I was right about one thing, but it wasn't the transition to our new lives in the city of New York. I was wrong about that. The reality was none of us, not my family nor the people who had relatives living in the US at the time, knew much about the massive size of this country and all of its fifty states. The only people who knew exactly where families or individuals were going to live in America were those responsible for accepting them into the refugee resettlement program. I have no doubt people had paperwork with names of cities and states they were going, but it's difficult to fully grasp the nature of a place you've never seen before. In our case, we were assigned to Buffalo, New York—a city I'd never heard of and knew nothing about. But because most people were familiar with New York we all assumed we were going to live in New York City. I did not know about New York State, the Empire State, and I didn't know there were other cities outside of the Big Apple until we landed in Buffalo.

When we stepped out of the plane at JFK everything around us seemed to move so fast there was no time to take in the fact we were now on American soil. We had to follow the groups of people ahead of us in hopes of figuring out how to navigate through whatever processes and procedures lay ahead. Fortunately along the way, there was a case worker waiting to greet and guide us through immigration and customs services. Thank God for that person, and for all the other case workers who are committed to assisting families like mine. US customs and immigration services can often be quite challenging and overwhelming for newcomers to navigate, especially if they don't speak English.

Imagine having to navigate a complicated immigration system in a foreign land you've never been in before, and in a language you do not speak or understand. Imagine having to go through that experience in one of the busiest and fastest moving environments in the world. Imagine trying to navigate that process with four young children by your side after a transcontinental flight spanning over twelve hours in the sky from Africa to the Americas. Imagine the amount of stress that comes with not knowing what do in that situation. That is exactly what my mom and stepfather were likely thinking about on the plane, and it seemed pretty apparent seconds after we stepped out of that aircraft.

A little bit of weight lifted from their shoulders the moment our case worker approached us and explained they were there to help guide and assist us through our transition. The relief on their faces was clear, and I can tell they were very appreciative even though we all understood hardly any of what was said by the case worker.

Thankfully we made it through the immigration and customs process without any issues and had to wait for the next step out of the airport. I remember there were two families traveling alongside us, one was a Sudanese family we knew from Egypt and the other was a Somali family we met at the airport in Cairo. The Sudanese family ended up on the same flight with us to Buffalo, but the Somali family of roughly ten individuals, a mother and her eight or nine children were heading to the great state of Texas.

While we all waited for the next step in our journey, I sparked a random conversation in Arabic with some of the Somali kids. That was the second time I heard anyone talk about this place called Texas. The first time was in Cairo when my friend and schoolmate by the name Kennedy told me he and his family were moving to a place called Texas in America. Sadly, he and I lost touch shortly after that conversation when they left Egypt, and we haven't spoken since. Interestingly enough, not long after our brief conversation about the state of Texas, the Somali kids and their Mom went their separate way and that was also the last time we saw each other. I sometimes wonder where they may have ended up in Texas, and how their lives might have turned out. It's been over twenty years since that day at JFK but I hope they were able to make the best of their newfound lives in the "land of opportunity." I hope they were all able to succeed in whatever path life may have taken them, and I hope they were able to live their version of the "American Dream."

DESTINATION: BUFFALO

The first time I stepped onto the streets of New York was to board an airport shuttle out of JFK. The shuttle transported us from the international arrival terminal through the streets of the city to our next destination. I remember thinking this was it, we were headed to our new apartment building somewhere in this massive and beautiful city, and I couldn't wait to see what it looked like.

I kept wondering how this day would end as I continued to stare out of the shuttle window fascinated by the countless skyscrapers off in the distance. Although I've become familiar with the sight of tall buildings over the past year or so living in Cairo, the buildings in New York City looked quite different. They were taller, designed differently, and were not clustered together in a similar fashion as those in Cairo.

The further we drove away from the airport, the more excited I was about what lay ahead. I kept thinking we are almost at our destination, and I knew exactly the first thing

I would do once we got there. My first act at the apartment was going to be taking off my new leather shoes I had been wearing for nearly twenty-four hours and were killing my feet. I've been so focused on all the new experiences around me that I managed to ignore the worsening pain on my feet for hours. I was starting to feel very uncomfortable and I needed to take them off as soon as possible. I thought about doing so on the shuttle but hesitated because I didn't want to get in trouble for delaying the driver once we'd reached out destination.

When the shuttle finally stopped it wasn't in front of an apartment building or even in a residential neighborhood. It stopped in front of a structure that appeared to be an entry point at another airport. We were instructed to grab our belongings which consisted of nothing more than my mom's purse, a diaper or baby bag for my sister, and the light blue plastic bag from the UNHCR's resettlement program. That bag contained all of our immigration documents and important paperwork for our new lives in America.

UNHCR is an acronym for the United Nations High Commissioner for Refugees commonly known as the UN Refugee Agency.[11] They are the organization that helped my family and I resettle in the United States, and the same organizations that has helped tens of thousands of individuals and families out of conflict zones throughout the world for decades.

The UNHCR does much more in addition to helping with refugee resettlement. Refugee resettlement is described as "the transfer of refugees from an asylum country to another

---

11   "Frequently Asked Questions," *UNHCR The UN Refugee Agency USA*, *Accessed March 5, 2021.*

State that has agreed to admit them and ultimately grant them permanent residence. [12] UNHCR is mandated by its Statute and the UN General Assembly Resolutions to undertake resettlement as one of the three durable solutions."

Resettlement in recent years has become a controversial topic in many of the handful of countries that participate in UNHCR's resettlement program including the United States. [13] This can be attributed to the changing attitudes regarding domestic immigration policies as well as the unique nature of resettlement, in "that it is the only durable solution that involves the relocation of refugees from an asylum country to a third country. There were 20.4 million refugees of concern to UNHCR around the world at the end of 2019, but less than one per cent of refugees are resettled each year."

According to the agency only 3 percent, of UNHCR's budget comes from the UN; the remaining 97 percent comes from voluntary contributions from governments, corporations, and individual donors. UNHCR relies on donations to ensure it can respond whenever and wherever a crisis strikes. The reality is my family and I would not have made it from Egypt to the United States without the UNHCR, and this is also true for many other families and individuals who have resettled through the agency. In the late 1990s and early 2000s when we were resettled, the world was much different than it is now. According to Migration Policy Institute (MPI) a leading nonpartisan organization in the field of US and European migration policies, in the year 2000, there were 73,147 refugees admitted into the United States with an

---

12 "Resettlement," *UNHCR The UN Refugee Agency USA, Accessed March 5, 2021.*

13 "Resettlement," *UNHCR The UN Refugee Agency USA, Accessed March 5, 2021.*

annual ceiling of 90,000. [14] My family and I were amongst those refugees admitted into the US.

The need for resettling refugees has not subsided or disappeared since then. In fact, the opposite has occurred. The need has increased as a result of growing conflicts in many parts of the world during the last two decades. Since our arrival in the United States in 2000, there were three other years with higher numbers of refugee admissions. In 2009 there were 74,654 refugees admitted, in 2010 there were 73,311 admitted, and 2016 had the highest number among all three years with 84,995 refugee admissions. The year 2016 also happened to be the only year that nearly reached the highest ceiling of more the seventy thousand admissions since 1992 when the United States last admitted 132,531 refugees, exceeding its ceiling of 132,000 for the year. In the three years prior to 2016, the US nearly reached its ceiling of 70,000 in 2013 with 69,926 admissions, in 2014 with 69,987, and in 2015 with 69,933 refugees admitted.

LAGUARDIA AIRPORT—GOODBYE NYC

After leaving JFK and shuttling across town to what seemed to be another airport, we entered what I now know to be LaGuardia Airport. I was a bit puzzled and confused as to why we were at another airport instead of our new apartment somewhere in the city. Having just spent over twelve hours on a plane, I wasn't excited about the idea of boarding another flight for an unknown number of hours to God knows where.

Shortly after arriving at LaGuardia, we went through US airport security for the first time and on to the terminal

---

14   "US Annual Refugee Resettlement Ceilings and Number of Refugees Admitted, 1980-Present," MPI, *Accessed March 5, 2021.*

with the scheduled flight to Buffalo, New York. This was before Transportation Security Administration (TSA) was founded and airport security procedures were different and much simpler. After waiting at the gate for about an hour, we started boarding. The first thing I noticed upon entering the cabin was the size of the aircraft. It seemed so much smaller than the massive international aircraft we boarded in Cairo, which was likely a Boeing 747. However, on this much smaller plane everything seemed to be more organized and moved faster. It seemed like clockwork compared to our boarding process in Cairo less than twenty-four hours prior.

As we prepare for departure, I heard the voice of a flight attend over the passenger address (PA) system, which took me by complete surprise. It suddenly occurred to me we were no longer in an Arabic-speaking country or part of the world. For the first time in my life, I was no longer in Sudan, Egypt, or on the African continent. I was now halfway across the world in an English-speaking country, where everything I saw in writing or heard spoken was in this new foreign language.

This was the first time I was hearing the English language being spoken fluently all around me, and for all of us really, with the possible exception of my stepdad. He was a teacher back in Sudan and grew up in South Sudan where the English language was a part of the school curriculum. But my mother, my siblings, and I did not have the same experience. However, in Cairo I was enrolled in school for about six or seven months before leaving Egypt for America. During that time, I did manage to learn a few basic English phrases and a handful of letters and numbers from the Arabic-English evening classes I attended.

TRAUMA FROM GRADE FIVE

Reflecting on those days in class is a bit tricky because every time I think about it, I'm conflicted. When I do, I'm not sure whether to be upset or to simply laugh and brush it off as just one of those crazy things that happened to me in Egypt. Regardless of how I deal with it, it certainly remains a traumatic experience that's difficult to forget because of a single incident.

It happened during one of my evening classes at school in *Sakakini* just a few months before moving to Buffalo. We had a number of teachers who taught different subjects such as Arabic, English, math, science, history, and geography. I was in grade five at the time and did pretty well on all subjects accept English. It proved to be a tough subject not only for me, but also for most of the other students because we had hardly any exposure to the subject back home in Sudan.

Most of the students in my class were born and raised in Khartoum, and our public education system was built around Arabic. There were of course private schools that offered foreign languages such as English and French, but few students were able to afford school fees for private education. I was in the fourth grade when my family left Sudan, and I don't remember having any exposure to another language besides Arabic in school.

When I started attending fifth grade at *Sakakini* I was excited about the new curricula. When I started learning my "A, B, Cs" and "1, 2, 3s" I really started to like my new school because English was always regarded as a special language even back home in Sudan. I remember how excited some Egyptians in my neighborhood would react when my answer to their constant question; *"bit calum engileze?"* was *"Au!"* meaning "You speak English?" to which I answered, "Yes." At eleven, I thought every day I learned something new in my English class qualified as "speaking the language." In reality, however, the only English phrases I could recite with confidence were ones I picked up listening to my teacher demonstrate in class, eavesdropping on English speakers at the church, and what I could recall from watching American movies on TV.

I learned phrases like, *What's your name? My name is...,* and *Where are you from?* That was enough to fascinate my Egyptian buddies and whenever they asked for more English, I would add the "A, B, Cs" and "1, 2, 3s" to end the free English session. However that was short-lived because my confidence in my newfound abilities to add a third language to my arsenal of multilingualism was shattered one evening during my English class.

Our teacher posed one question, and one question only which put the entire class on edge. Well, almost the entire class. There was one student who turned out to know the correct answer and that student later made a terrible example out of the rest of us. The teacher wrote two English numbers on the chalkboard, the number seven and the number eleven. He then asked which number was which? When he first raised the question, he looked around the class in hopes of seeing one or more hands raised to answer the question. Not a single hand went up. He waited a few seconds and once again asked with a more intense demeanor "Which number is seven and which number is eleven?" Once again, no one volunteered to step up to provide an answer.

This was pretty unusual because there were always at least one or two students, me included who normally jumped at the chance to answer. It was usually an opportunity for some students to show off their level of intellect in front of the whole class, but for some reason this time no one dared.

The teacher decided to pose the question a third time which was rare to begin with, but changed the format to compel all of us to choose one or the other. This was his way of guaranteeing there will not be a fourth opportunity for any student to answer the question. We knew exactly how he operated from past experience in his classroom. He proceeded and asked for the final time, "If you think this is the number seven raise your hand," pointing at the number seven. "If you think this is the number seven raise your hand," and pointed at the number eleven.

The entire class froze for a second, myself included, and that's when I realized we were confused by the similarity of the words seven and eleven. None of us felt confident answering the question straight forward. Secondly, every student knew the teacher was frustrated with the direction of the lesson so far, and if you were to take a chance and answered wrong, you will surely suffer a consequence. No one in the class wanted to be that student no one wanted to take the fall for the entire class.

Finally, it was time to choose your answer and lock it in. He pointed to the number eleven and said, "If you think this is seven raise your hand." We all felt the pressure and began raising our hands one after another like a chain reaction. I wasn't sure if the answer was correct, but as more hands went up, I started to feel confidant and also raised my hand. I thought surely we couldn't all be wrong.

From their faces, you could see all the other students were beginning to feel confident in their choice to follow suit and agree the number we all were looking at was indeed the number seven and not eleven. All of us in class had our hands up and were feeling good about it, except one student. He kept his hand down, eyes locked on the chalkboard, and didn't bother to look at anyone else. I was sitting just a few feet from him and wondered along with the rest of the class what was going on in his head.

The teacher glanced at the one student who did not raise his hand along with the rest of us, and after a few seconds decided to proceed to the second part of the question. He then said pointing to the number seven "If you think this is the number seven raise your hand." We all put our hands down and only one hand went up. A few of the kids looked at one another and started to chuckle a little bit. The rest of us looked around at each other with anticipation wondering what was going to happen next. Who answered correctly? Did the overwhelming majority of the class answer correctly or did one student know something we didn't?

As we continued to wait for the teacher to reaffirm who answered correctly, time seemed to slow down a bit. When he finally affirmed the correct answer, twenty-nine of the thirty students in class were shocked. The teacher wasted no time showing his disapproval and immediately called up the one student to the front of the class. He then handed him the ruler he used to both teach and discipline students.

At that point it was clear the kid was the only student who correctly identified the difference between the number seven and the number eleven. I remember looking at both the teacher and my classmates and thinking "I can't believe we all answered wrong and only one of us answered right." I was shocked, in disbelief and frankly disappointed in myself but there was no time for self-pity. Every student in class was probably feeling the same way and we all knew the teacher had plans to discipline the rest of us for this massive failure. We suspected he had something up his sleeve but no one knew for sure what it was given the number of students who answered wrong. Every student probably thought there were way too many of us for the teacher to discipline us one at a time, and we were right.

We were right to a certain extent. He was not intent on disciplining all twenty-nine of us one by one, instead, he passed that responsibility to one student. At first, I was relieved and thought, *okay, that's not the worst thing that can happen and it's certainly not as bad as I thought it was going be.* We knew the teacher had a heavy hand, but he was an adult so that's to be expected. This student was a kid just like the rest of us. Besides, he was a classmate and I was sure he was going to take it easy on us just like any other student would do for their classmates.

I have never been more wrong in my life. This kid had no intentions of taking it easy on anyone nor did he seemed to care about making friends or enemies that day. He took this job like an opportunity to punish all of us for a crime we didn't know was committed against him. I remember the teacher giving him the ruler and asking every other student to line up in a single file. We had to stick our palms out in front of this kid and he struck every student with the same intensity and force one after another. He didn't seem to care whether you were a boy, girl, someone he knew and spoke with regularly or sat next to in class.

I didn't know him personally at the time but I'd seen him outside of class occasionally. I knew some of his family members from Sunday mass and other church activities but not on a personal level. Needless to say, we were all shocked about what transpired in that classroom and many of the students didn't associate with him after day. Others stopped talking with him completely, myself included, because we were so angry with him. I couldn't believe he didn't bother to show any shred of mercy to his own classmates. I thought this kid had serious issues for what he did and I just kept my distance from him for the rest of the year. For me, the only good thing that came out of that experience was a reminder to never make that mistake again. I made sure to study harder and to be extra smart and careful about answering any questions posed in that class until we left Egypt.

The irony about that traumatic experience was the fact this kid along with his family later boarded the same flight with my family to America. He and I boarded the same flight from Cairo International Airport to JFK International Airport as well as the same flight from LaGuardia to Buffalo-Niagara International Airport. We were even once again classmates a few years after resettling in Buffalo. This time however, my English language skills were far superior. It's hard to believe but he and I even managed to become close friends in high school. Our families grew closer over the first few years in Buffalo, and so did our friendship. But I still haven't forgotten that traumatic incident even though it's been over twenty years. I'm sure however, my friend Samson knows I have already forgiven him for that incident a long time ago.

CHAPTER 14

Buffalo, New York

The flight from New York City to Buffalo was about an hour long. We landed at the Buffalo-Niagara International Airport a lot sooner than I had anticipated which was great news. I was concerned our second flight might end up in the sky for a few hours before reaching our destination and I was already feeling a bit jetlagged. As we prepared for landing, I looked out the window and noticed how much smaller the airport was compared to JFK and LaGuardia. I did not see any large planes similar to the one we arrived on from Egypt, and we were able to exit the plane into the terminal much faster than at JFK. I was happy about the short flight duration, but anxious to see what happened next.

Everything around us still seemed to be moving fast, but not at the same pace as in JFK or LaGuardia. A few minutes after we exited the flight we were greeted by a gentleman from Catholic Charities. He introduced himself as a caseworker assigned to assist my family and make sure we arrived in one piece. He directed us to baggage claim to collect our belongings, and after we picked up our luggage it was time to leave the airport.

The car ride to our new home was quite interesting. My mom, stepdad and my sister, Adut, were seated in the second row of the minivan and my brothers and I were seated in the third. The drive from the airport was no longer than twenty to twenty-five minutes and I spent the entire ride staring out the window fascinated with everything I saw. The first thing that caught my attention was how green everything seemed. I had never seen so many trees on the side of the road before and they all looked beautiful and well kept. The second thing I noticed was the clear blue sky above and the quiet, clean, and colorful vehicles driving past us on the road. No dust, mud, or damage on any of them which was something I wasn't accustomed to seeing in Cairo. Lastly, the houses looked strange and built right next to the road. I wondered why they were so close to each other and why none of them had any walls built around them like the rich neighborhoods in Cairo or even the poor ones in Sudan.

We finally reached the house, our new home, on the city's westside neighborhood after an interesting drive through some of Buffalo's main roads. I remember it as if it was yesterday—a beautiful, calm, and quiet afternoon. We got there late afternoon around 4:00–4:30 p.m. The sun was still shining with a pleasant 75 to 80-degree temperature and it felt amazing. We stopped on the side of the road in front of a small house. It was a white house with two floors. On the right side of it there were two other structures one was another small house and the other appeared to be some sort of establishment. It was a high-end restaurant but didn't look like one to me that particular day. To the left of our new home was a three- to four-story brick building with a vacant lot next to it. It was also vacant and appeared to have experienced a terrible fire that destroyed everything within it.

Our case worker seemed familiar with the neighborhood and comfortable with everything we were trying to take in.

He made his way up the steps of the porch and unlocked the front door while my stepdad and I started unloading our luggage. For a moment, I looked around in attempt to survey the rest of our new neighborhood before walking into the house for the first time. As I gazed around slowly for a second, I couldn't help but notice there was no one else besides us in sight. I looked down both ends of the street and I couldn't see anyone walking, standing around, or even children playing outside. I could only see a few cars passing by on the main road a few blocks away which was such a strange and unusual sight.

In Egypt you couldn't step outside of your apartment building on to the street without seeing a bunch of people. There were always children playing or hanging out near their buildings. Sometimes you could hear them before seeing them running down the street shouting and screaming about something. Using an inside voice wasn't really a thing in Egypt, and that's just how it was. Everyone always felt the need to speak loudly or yell all the time for some reason. It takes a while to get used to such an environment, but eventually it starts to seem normal. However, once you're in a completely different environment that seems to be the total opposite of it, you began to appreciate the lack of chaos.

Welcome to your new home were the next words I remember hearing when we first entered our new apartment. The caseworker showed us around the two-bedroom upstairs apartment before he said goodbye and left for the day. He started with the kitchen which was the first place visible when entering the apartment. Immediately to the left of the front door was the restroom, and next to it was the fridge, kitchen sink and cabinets against the wall. The fridge was filled with all kinds of food like fruits, vegetables, meats, milk cheese and many other items. Across from it on the opposite end of the kitchen was a small kitchen table with nonrefrigerated food items. There were boxes of snacks, bags of potato chips, soda cans, but my favorite was the freshly baked French baguettes. I loved bread. Next, my brothers and I got a tour of our shared room before we moved on to the living room and my parents' bedroom.

My brothers and I were extremely excited about having a bedroom we could call our own. First, we'd never had a space of our own before then. In Sudan, we all lived in one small room we shared with our parents, and in Cairo we didn't have a room at all. The room our parents were in, along with our newborn sister, was way too small even just for the three of them. That's why my two little brothers and I slept in the living room in the tiny apartment until we left for America.

My excitement wasn't necessarily about the fact we finally had a room of our own, it had more to do with a feeling of gratitude. I was grateful to have something I never had before and didn't even know I needed until that point. I turned eleven years old the month before we arrived in Buffalo and until that point, I thought only adults were allowed to have a room of their own. I thought kids had to always share whatever space was available with their parents.

The next day the case worker showed up to pick us up for our first appointment at the Catholic Charities center. My parents had meetings with caseworkers and other people working and volunteering to help new refugee families settle into the community. The center also offered educational programs for adults who did not speak the English language called Parent Center as well as daycare services for kids. My brothers and I spent a good amount of time at the center during our first few months in Buffalo because we arrived at the closing end of the school year. Buffalo's school calendar year runs from September to June and we arrived in late April of that school year. We had to wait until the next school calendar year, from September 2000 to June 2001 to enroll.

I really wanted to start school right away but I wasn't bothered by how things started out. I had lots of fun at Catholic Charites and I used to enjoy watching cartoons and educational shows like Barney & Friends and Sesame Street. As far as I was concerned, I had an extra two months of summer to get comfortable in my new hometown, and an opportunity to learn a bit of the English language before starting school. I could say it worked out in my favor.

Buffalo had already welcomed a number of Sudanese refugee families into the community by the time we arrived. Many of those families had children across the age spectrum just like my siblings and I. Luckily for us, one of those families lived nearby on the next block. I remember they were the first couple that visited just days after we had settled in and their house was about a three-minute walk from ours. The lady was really nice and instantly hit it off with my mother, and her husband was pretty friendly as well. They had a daughter who was roughly the same age as my middle brother Aken. Within a few weeks we were regularly going over to their house to hang out and watch cable TV. While our parents spent their time exchanging stories about life in Sudan, Egypt, and America so far, we were busy watching Cartoon Network.

Within those first few weeks a second family visited. They lived just a few blocks from our house. The parents were soft-spoken and gentle, traits they clearly passed down to their children. The oldest was a boy my age he introduced himself as Oscar but the rest of the family regularly called him, "*Tabule*" which was his home name. The other two children were Nancy and Francis, and both were about the same age as my siblings Aken and Moum. I remember the first time Oscar and I met and little did I know that was the beginning of friendship and a brotherhood that would last over twenty years and counting.

There were other Sudanese families that visited and welcomed us into the Buffalo-Sudanese community over the next few months over the summer. Chief amongst them was the Simon Mut family. They lived many blocks away from us but on the same side of town. Their house seemed very far away and much further than Oscar's house. But they too, had children my age, my brother Aken's age, and my youngest brother Moum's age. The oldest son Mut was a lively character and whenever we visited their house he always had something new and different to introduce us to. The second oldest boy Dew was pretty calm and collected and always had a smile on his face. It was always a good time hanging out with them whenever the opportunity presented itself.

I remember the first time we were invited over to their house for a birthday party. There were a bunch of other Sudanese kids there as well. It was during a nice summer evening and we played outside in the small from yard for a while before dinner time and pizza was on the menu. I had never eaten pizza before in my life, and I wasn't sure what to expect. However, Mut raved about the dish and managed to convince me it was the best thing since sliced bread. So I agreed and said I would give it a try.

We all went inside the house and got a slice or two of cheese pizza. At first, I wasn't impressed with the way it looked. The aroma of the melted cheese was very unusual and foreign to me. The only cheese I was familiar with was

Feta cheese. It was the only cheese I used to eat with *Ful Medames* (fava beans) both in Sudan and Egypt.

After I took my first bite of cheese pizza, I started struggling trying to keep it down and not vomit. Immediately I thought to myself, *why would anyone in their right mind eat this*? I had never in my life eaten so much cheese at once and my belly didn't know how to process it. The only time I remember feeling anything remotely close to how I felt after that first bite was during my childhood in Sudan when I attempted to drink milk. No matter how hard I tried, I simply couldn't digest cow, sheep, or even goat milk during those days. So I completely stayed away and stopped trying to drink milk from that point on. I honestly kept my distance from milk and most dairy products like yogurt and anything with a strong dairy scent to it.

I didn't start trying to consume dairy products again until I was introduced to cereal and milk, and then introduced to chocolate milk in the sixth grade. Needless to say, I did not finish that slice of pizza at Mut's party, and I didn't attempt to eat another slice of pizza until I started to slowly warm up to cheese and peperoni at school.

The summer of 2000 was interesting and memorable, and I was really happy about meeting lots of Sudanese kids my age and their families. I'm glad to have met Oscar, Mut, Dew and their families that summer because they helped make the transition to life in this country so much easier. They became more than just friends they were my brothers, and the bond we developed over the years is still strong until this very day. It's hard to believe but it's been over two decades since that first summer. Life has taken us all into different directions over those years but thinking about those days always brings back fond memories.

Memories of our short-lived childhood years in Buffalo may have seemed trivial at the time but were important and monumental moments we shared. I can still recall a lot of the first things that happened that year—the first church we attended at the invitation of Oscar and his family, the first Christmas party we experienced with Mut and his family, and the first community gathering we were a part of with many other Sudanese families. Those days helped make life seemed normal for kids our age during a period of time that was anything but normal. All of our families were in the midst of rebuilding their lives in a broader community that wasn't our own, in a foreign country and land that wasn't our own.

PUBLIC SCHOOL INTERNATIONAL SCHOOL #45

In September of 2000, I started my first year of education in the English language at School 45. Officially known as Public School 45 International School it is one of the most diverse primary and middle schools in the city of Buffalo. I was enrolled into the sixth grade along with many other international students from all over the globe who attended School 45. There were kids from virtually every continent walking the halls which truly made it international. It also made being the new kid much easier because I didn't have to try very hard to fit it, make new friends or feel out of place and unwelcomed.

The language barrier was a bit difficult to deal with in the beginning but being at an international school was great because there were programs available to help make the transition easier for new students like myself. There were programs such as English as a Second Language (ESL) classes and a diverse staff of teachers and aids with different backgrounds. There were also a number of Sudanese and other students form Arabic-speaking countries in many of my classes. They sometimes helped translate what I did not quite understand which made a difference during the first few months.

I was also determined to improve my English-speaking skills and did not want to fall behind my classmates. It didn't matter to me whether English was your first and only language, or whether it was your second, third, or fourth. I knew I could learn it just as fast and easily as the next student I just had to try my best.

Within three months or so of the school year, I was able to speak English fluently. Literacy was a different topic, but I was confident my reading and writing skills would follow in time. My teachers where extremely helpful and patient with me during those first months, and it quickly became apparent to me how different the educational system was between the US, Sudan and Egypt.

I was accustomed to school systems that were quite strict and rigid both in Khartoum and Cairo, and to teachers who scared you into learning. Fear of failure and the harsh disciplinary measures students faced were central parts of those educational systems. Here in America however, it was a completely different model.

One of the first things I noticed at School 45 was the more soft and gentle approach teachers used to deal with students. For instance, when a student completed a task or answered a question correctly, they were rewarded with a compliment or a good job. When they did not or happened to answer incorrectly, they weren't punished for it. They were let down easily and encouraged to do better next time. Sometimes the teacher even helped them figure out the correct answer or provided it to the entire class.

I was shocked the first time I saw that happening and thought, What? That's the strangest thing ever. Teachers don't let you off the hook that easily. Also, they do not pay you compliments for answering questions correctly, and if they did, it is rare because it is expected of us. That's what students do! The first week or two of school I noticed none of the teachers disciplined students for misbehaving the same way teachers did in Sudan or Egypt—not with a ruler, a stick, or some other kind of *soth* (whip).

I later learned it's not a common practice in this part of the world. Teachers do not put hands on students for misbehaving or for any other reason. If students were misbehaving in class, teachers used verbal warnings and threats to send them to the principal's office. This was strange but interesting and great news to me personally. The fact I did not have to worry about corporal punishment at school was excellent, but I was still curious about what happens in the principal's office. I of course had no intentions of misbehaving or taking advantage, but I was curious to know about the worst-case scenario once the principal was involved.

FIRST FALL AND WINTER SEASONS

Everything seemed to be going well at school but similar to the changing autumn weather in Buffalo, things at home were beginning to take a turn. A couple of months after our arrival my stepdad started working and my mother stayed home with us. My baby sister, Adut, was just over a year old and my mom was pregnant with my brother Mondot. By this point my stepdad, Natale, managed to save up enough money to purchase a car. He bought a small, white, two-door Coupe similar to a 1990 Model Ford Escort or a Honda Integra. This meant he no longer had to carpool with his new friend, our

Sudanese neighbor who worked with him at a meat plant near downtown Buffalo.

As the fall season fast approached, the temperatures gradually dropped and the tree leaves started to change colors. Within a matter of weeks the trees shifted from having beautiful autumn-colored leaves to having no leaves at all. This transition was amazing to watch because I had never seen anything like it before. Although the temperatures were noticeably getting colder, I wasn't bothered and did not think much of it at first. In Egypt, I had experienced a similar shift in the weather for the first time during the winter season the year before. I had to wear a winter jacket for a few months in Cairo and I suspected it was going to be the same, or a similar scenario this time around. Boy was I wrong.

It had been about six or seven months since we moved to Buffalo and my role and responsibilities as the oldest boy in the family had not changed. The only difference was I no longer had to prepare my siblings for school every morning and walk them down to *Sakakini* as I did in Egypt. I also didn't have to watch my infant sister all day while my parents were at work. I didn't have to go pick up the kids from school or head back out the door for my evening classes as I did before. I was now a regular eleven-year-old kid with an eleven-year-old schedule consisting of going to school, doing homework, and figuring out things to do with the free time I now had.

I still had to run errands like going to the neighbors or to the nearby corner store to pick up whatever Mom needed that day. I was happy to do it, had no complaints, and was pleased with the outcome of this new arrangement. On the weekends, we usually had a chance to hang out with my new friends Oscar and Mut on Saturdays, and Sunday mornings we regularly attended church.

Life seemed pretty good at that point and felt like a major upgrade compared to Egypt. But like all good things, the grace period ended. In late October or early November, temperatures started dropping even further and I wasn't sure what to make of it. The sky regularly started to seem more gray all the time and the days seemed shorter and got darker way sooner than months before. Now there were even days the sun did not appear at all and not just for a day or two, but for three and four days at a time. It was weird and I didn't like it.

One day, all of the sudden, I saw what appeared to be tiny little cotton balls falling from the sky outside the window. It started to happen around four or five in the evening and I remember that strange day very well. We were already back home from school and Aken, Moum, and I were sitting in the living room watching TV. I first noticed this phenomenon start to take place from a distance away. I was seated on the sofa across the room roughly ten to twelve feet from the TV set, and behind it there were three large windows with blinds which were partly raised.

Through the windows I could see it was beginning to get dark outside but it wasn't yet as dark as the night sky. As my brother and I continued to watch TV, I noticed something falling outside from the sky, but it didn't look or sound like rain. I then got off my seat and walked to the window for a closer look. Immediately I called my brothers over to come look at this strange white rain falling in slow motion from the sky.

The next morning when we were preparing to go to school I saw the snow-covered ground outside the house. It was a sight like nothing I had ever seen everything appeared bright white and it was a fascinating experience. I reached down and touched snow for the first time and it was soft, fluffy, and felt cold like ice when it melts.

Days after the first snow fall it no longer appeared soft, fluffy, and magical. It also didn't feel as interesting to touch with my barehand like the first time, and certainly not after the day I experienced frost bite. The road in front of the house started to look a bit dirty from cars driving by and the sidewalk was also starting to look the same due to foot traffic. I had a bike by that time and I looked forward to every opportunity to take it for spin because I hadn't been allowed to go outside much or ride around the neighborhood since I got it. The only other time I could take my bike for a ride was whenever I was sent to the corner store. There were a few corner stores in the neighborhood but I regularly went to one store at the end of our block.

One particularly cold and snowy day, I was sent to buy some household item for my mother. Like always, I jumped at the opportunity to get on my bike and ride down to the store. I put on my winter coat and boots and out the door I went. I did not however, have on any winter gloves. It was snowing outside but not very heavy and visibility was decent. I was mindful of the fact riding my bike in the snow was not the same as on a clear road, and I knew I needed to be more careful. I did not think much about the danger posed by the wet snow falling on my bare hands.

By the time I got to the store my hands felt a little bit wet and cold, but I simply wiped them off and proceeded to buy what Mom requested from the store. I then got back on my bike about five minutes later and started heading home. When I came out of the store, I didn't look like anything had changed during the five minutes or so I was inside the store. My hands felt a bit warmer since I did try to warm them up while waiting in line at the store to cash out.

Halfway down the block and just a few minutes from home I started to feel a tingling sensation in all my fingers. It also seemed to intensify with every passing second. I quickly decided it was best to start peddling faster so I could get home sooner and put a stop to this terrible feeling. The problem with that logic proved to be the faster I peddled my bike, the more intense the tingling felt. My knuckles started to feel like someone was slicing through them with a sharp knife. As all these things were happening all at once, the snow fall was starting to interfere with the visibility of the street.

The wind was on my back when I went to the store, which helped me get there much faster without any issues. But on my way back from the store, I was riding my bike against that same wind. The wind was working against me this time around and blowing snow in my face, onto my hands, and ripping into my bare knuckles. When I finally got home, I picked up my bike and walked up the steps onto the porch and dropped it there. I then grabbed the plastic bag I was holding with all the items I bought and ran up the stairs into the apartment.

While running up the flight of stairs my hands were freezing and had a burning sensation at the same time. I was struggling to process and understand how that could be and what could be done to stop it. First thing I did when I made it through the apartment door was to immediately drop the plastic bag. Second thing, I ran into the bathroom and turned on the hot water. You can take a wild guess as to what I did next.

If you guessed I stuck my hands into the hot water, you are correct. I absolutely did, and the feeling of relief I was so sure would follow did not come. I thought, *This is it. My hands are done and going to fall of my wrist.* I was terrified and genuinely afraid of not having any functional hands for the rest of my life.

Thankfully my hands did not fall off my wrist. Instead, I got a bitter taste of what it feels like to suffer frostbite for the first time. I learned a valuable lesson that day. The lesson was to stay inside and hibernate all winter if possible. Don't go outside when the trees are bare and have no leaves, and most importantly, do not—I repeat, do not—ride a bike during the winter months. Period.

That was my first horrific winter experience in Buffalo and as much as I would love to say it was my only one, it was not. However, first experiences often leave bigger impressions on must people and I can say for certain the first winter left a big negative impression on me. I hated winter for a long time and still struggle with it today.

CHAPTER 15

Like Weather, People Change

———

The first winter was tough on all of us, including my parents. During those winter months, my mom and stepdad started to argue a lot and I took notice. It wasn't my first time to seeing it happen, but before moving to Buffalo it was rare to see them fight and argue. I'm sure it happened, all parents argue and I was old enough to know that. It just never happened in front of us. My brothers Aken and Moum were younger at the time, and they may not recall these events happening as vividly as I did, but it was very unusual and difficult to witness.

Back home in Khartoum living together with my grandparents, aunts and uncles meant there were other adults in the home to help resolve whatever issues families had. If there was problem family members from both sides could step in and help mediate to find a resolution. In Egypt it wasn't quite the same but we lived with Natale's friend and his family, and there were other relatives and family friends available to step in as well. But in Buffalo we didn't have that same support system. We didn't have relatives or close family friends.

I was aware at that age children did not have any role to play in such matters. At such a young age my only duty was to obey my parents and do whatever they asked of me. I did exactly that most of the time. However, there was a point when I could not continue to force myself to ignore the increasing tension between my mom and stepdad. Their fights were becoming more and more frequent and on full display before my young siblings and me. It became almost routine and I knew what was going to happen as soon as my stepdad came home drunk after having a few too many beers with his work buddies. He would immediately start a fight with Mom.

This behavior continued for a while until it reached the point I just couldn't stand it anymore. I felt I had to stand up for my mom and do something about my stepdad's unacceptable and abusive behavior. During those days Mom kept to herself and didn't say much. On the other hand, Natale didn't know when to quit. He would go on and on verbally abusing my mom until tears began to run down her cheeks. At first, I couldn't believe what was happening and didn't understand how Natale, a man I've known virtually my entire life could do this to her. I struggled to understand who he had become, and what caused him to all of the sudden turn into this toxic figure.

For as long as I've known him, Natale has always been the quite type who mostly kept to himself. He met my mother in the early '90s when I was about two years old. They started a family soon after and my brother Aken was born in 1992. From that point on he's been in my life and lived with us in my grandparent's home in *Shigla, Haj Yousif* until we left for Egypt in 1999. He was accepted into our family and respected by everyone in the household and throughout the community. My grandpa called him *Jal-pownye* which means teacher in *Cøllø* because he worked as a teacher at the local Comboni school which I also attended.

At the school he was also the artistic illustrator and created academic artwork for other primary schools in our neighborhood. He drew amazing pictures and Arabic letters used to teach kids like me the alphabet in primary school. That's the man I knew him to be, respected, and accepted into my life all those years. To see him now mistreating my mother, the woman I hold near and dear to my heart, was beyond belief. It was shocking, confusing, and felt like the ultimate act of betrayal by someone I once and considered to be a father figure. He was someone I genuinely believed to be a good person.

I decided to get involved one day when I genuinely felt afraid for my mom and concerned about her safety. I felt could no longer be a bystander and continue to watch what was happening in front of me. Most Sudanese children are raised to respect their parents and elders at all times. They are raised to never talk back to an adult and to never equate themselves to their elders. These are simply things children in Sudanese society do not do, and any attempt to break those rules are considered to be disrespectful and outrageous. However, I had no other option but to act that day.

It was a Saturday evening and we were all at home watching TV while Mom prepared dinner. I was watching my baby sister Adut and my brothers Aken and Moum were sitting beside me in the living room. Natale didn't work during the weekends and usually went out drinking with his friends. When he came home that evening after having a few too many beers, my mother was not in the house. She stepped out just a minutes before and went to the neighbor's house to pick up something. By the time she returned home ten to fifteen minutes later, Natale was waiting to greet her with some harsh and unpleasant words.

He was clearly angry with my mom and made it very clear as soon as she walked in through the door. This was not the first time I've seen him behave in that way, but the interesting thing about my stepdad is he only acted that way when he was drunk. When sober, the man was as cool as a cucumber and kept to himself most of the time. It took some time to understand how he functioned and what he was capable off under the influence, and the image I once had of him as a father figure slowly started to fade. A new one began to formulate and I started to see him for what he truly was.

That night the argument quickly escalated and turned fierce between the two of them like nothing I had ever seen before. My siblings and I were still sitting in the living room as we watched our parents fight before our eyes. As the situation continued to intensify, my sister Adut started to cry. She was just over a year old at the time and I had to hold her in my arms to try calming her down. My bothers Aken and Moum watched from a distance not knowing how to react or what to do.

At one point during the heated argument, things took a turn for the worst and my stepdad started to get physically aggressive. Seeing what was happening, I started to try and separate them with one hand and while still holding my sister Adut with the other. Drunk and out of control, Natale proceeded to violently push her against the living room wall, yelling and screaming at the top of his lungs. As I watched my mother frightened and scared for her life, struggle to break free from his grip I knew something major had to be done—and fast.

At eleven years old, I was barley five feet tall and weighted no more than one hundred pounds. Physically I was no match for a grown man acting violent during a drunken rage. I had already tried and was unable to successfully push Natale off my mom. I had to find another way to help my mom and I could not run to the neighbor's house for help because I didn't want to leave Mom alone with Natale. I couldn't send Aken eight at the time, out on his own because it was dark outside and frankly the idea never crossed my mind.

At this point the situation was getting dire. Natale grabbed some household item and struck my mom on her head as we all watched. I immediately ran picked up the house phone and called the police. I explained to the dispatch operator what was happening to my mother and pleaded for them to send emergency help right away. Thank God for the officers who responded to the domestic violence call because they arrived in a matter of minutes.

When the two police officers arrived, I ran downstairs to open the door and ran back upstairs to the apartment. Upon entering the apartment, the officers were able to quickly assess the situation and conclude Natale was the culprit. They instructed him to get up from his seat, to turn around, and place his hands behind his back before they cuffed him.

As the officers prepared to read Natale his Miranda Rights and haul him away, I interjected and started to explain why I called for help. I told them I only needed help breaking up the fight because I wasn't able to do so by myself with my little sister in my arms. I explained I didn't want them to take my parents away. I explained to them we were still new to Buffalo and I didn't know who else to call, and back home there were always family members around to help stop such behavior. The officers then warned and explained to Natale domestic violence is a serious crime in this country, and he would be arrested if it happened again. The heavy drinking hasn't stopped, but that was the first and last time he placed hands on my mother.

NEW NEIGHBORHOOD AND NEW ADVENTURES

In January of 2001, my brother Mondot was born. It was an exciting time for all of us to welcome a new member of the family. That same year however, my maternal grandmother passed away. I remember being with my mom at the time and she did not display much of the grief she was feeling, but I knew losing her mother was difficult. Mom was close with Grandma; I was also close with Grandma. She practically raised me along with my mom in Sudan and it was heartbreaking none of us had a chance to say our goodbyes.

Communication with family in Sudan was rare at the time and Mom tried her best to regularly stay in touch. She also tried hard to shield me from the sorrow she felt after losing Grandma and didn't talk much about it. Before we left Sudan, and for a good portion of my early childhood, I spent most of my time at home with my grandmother. She was a small woman in stature but commanded respect from everyone around her. You always respected Grandma if you knew what was good for you. I learned that lesson early on in my life. I was her only grandson running around for two to three years before my brother Aken was born and then Moum and our cousin Beta.

My grandmother's *Cøllø* name is *Nya-whi-deng* and her Christian name is Noel. I didn't call her by either; to me she was always *Haboba* or *Wongoo* which translates to grandma in Arabic and *Cøllø*. It's difficult express in simple words how much my grandmother meant to me. Losing her was hard to deal with, and is still difficult to think about to this day. What hurts the most is the fact I never had a chance to properly say goodbye, not even over the phone. I take solace in knowing she watches over me and continues to send her love and blessing from up above. I love you grandma; you will forever be missed.

During the early months of summer 2001, we moved from our first Buffalo apartment to our second. The new apartment was nearby and about three city blocks away from the old one. It was slightly larger and the new neighborhood had much more activity compared to the previous one. There was a lot more activity from our neighbors especially during the summer. The new apartment was directly across the street from not one but two community centers. There was a playground visible from my bedroom window, a swimming pool, and a basketball court directly behind the center.

The new place felt amazing because of what it had to offer compared to the old apartment. Even though they were technically in the same neighborhood, they offered two different experiences. We were still new to Buffalo at the time and I never quite ventured out into many other neighborhoods often so it was a bit surprising. I later learned more about the unique and interesting layout the city has compared to other similarly sized cities around the country. Buffalo happens to be one of the few places I've been where if you drive a few minutes in any direction, you're likely to find yourself in a completely different neighborhood.

A few months after we moved into the new apartment the school year ended. Before summer break, I had started attending one of the two community centers for the after-school programs they offered. It was a great place to receive extra help with homework, play basketball and other fun actives, as well as make new friends. A few of the kids I knew from school lived in the same area and we started hanging out more and more throughout those summer months. My friend Oscar and I, as well as another new friend named Diaa, spent lots of those summer days playing basketball.

Between basketball and hanging out at each other's home that summer, Oscar and I started practicing Capoeira two to three times a week. We didn't know anything about it at first but we were curious about the Brazilian dance-infused martial art. We were invited to join a class one day by one of the practitioners after they saw Oscar and I practicing handstands right outside the entrance near the playground. Out of curiosity we accepted to come see what Capoeira was and what it was all about.

During the first class we had a chance to grasp the basics of the martial art. I was personally intrigued by the more advanced skilled movements some of the seasoned practitioners displayed. I wanted to learn them and thought it would be really cool and fun to master a few moves.

Capoeira is an Afro-Brazilian martial art, sometimes described as a dance said to have originated in the sixteenth century. [15] The origins of Capoeira are said to be tied to the enslaved peoples taken from West Africa to the Portuguese colony, Brazil. Forbidden from practicing their cultures and any form of martial arts under the oppressing laws of the colonizers, Capoeira emerged as a way to circumvent those restrictions. With deep roots in Brazilian culture, this martial art in dance form survived through the centuries and would eventually become a world phenomenon.

---

15   Juan Goncalves-Borrega, "How Brazilian Capoeira Evolved From a Martial Art to an International Dance Craze," *Smithsonian Magazine,* September 21, 2017.

Most people who are into gaming are probably familiar with Eddy Gordo, the character from the video game Tekken. [16] Eddy is a Capoeirista, a Capoeira fighter, in the video game series and exemplifies the best of the best in the marital art. I began practicing Capoeira at age twelve and continued for a few years until the age of fourteen or fifteen. During those few years I learned a lot in terms of the martial art itself, and also about discipline and commitment. I was surrounded by really amazing people who helped me learn the art and excel at my strengths. At twelve, I was a flexible kid who loved learning flips and Capoeira moves involving lots of twists and turns. For that reason I was dubbed *ponte* my Capoeira name meaning bridge in Portuguese.

We lived in that apartment for two summers or rather two winters. I remember the winter months in more detail because half of the apartment did not have adequate heating. It was a two-bedroom upstairs apartment like our first apartment but only the living room, dining room, and one of the bedrooms had decent heating. The kitchen, bathroom, and the second bedroom were ice-cold all of the time. There was hardly any heat that reached the back of the unit for two years and it was dreadful having to go to the kitchen or bathroom.

The second bedroom in the unit was only useful during the summer months. During the winter, my siblings and I transformed the dining and living rooms into our sleeping quarters. It was a reminder of living conditions I had hoped we left behind in Egypt. It was upsetting because I'd grown accustomed to having a bedroom in our last apartment, and this new arrangement felt like a major setback.

---

16 "Eddy Gordo," Comic Vine, Accessed March 5, 2021.

My relationship with my stepfather Natale had further deteriorated at that point which didn't help matters much. I was now in the seventh grade and my English had dramatically improved. I had familiarized myself with the lay of the land and with how things were done in the American school system and I made sure to avoid any serious trouble for bad grades or misbehavior. As far as I was concerned, things were going well for me at school and I was happy about it. I also had new friends and got along with them very well. The only issues I was dealing with were at home and I didn't understand why my stepdad was being so difficult to deal with.

I thought I was a decent kid overall but for some reason Natale and I could not get along. I was convinced his aim was to try and make life hell not only for me, but for my mother as well. Although, during those two years their relationship didn't seem as volatile compared to our first year in Buffalo. It's possible things only seemed slightly better between them because I wasn't at home as much anymore to witness most of the chaos. It's also probable Natale simply started to redirect his anger and toxic behavior away from my mother and toward me instead.

Whatever the case may have been, the reality still showed not much had actually changed in our household. My stepdad was still a heavy drinker and his behavior remained the same when under the influence. He was still regularly verbally abusive toward my mom. The only difference was I was no longer a bystander and was old enough to standup and do something about it. I no longer felt he deserved my respect and I challenged him about his behavior every time. He hated that but I didn't care.

It quickly became apparent and didn't take very long before Natale started to show his disdain for me. At first, he took issue with some of my friends in the neighborhood and didn't want to see me with them. He didn't think it was a good idea to be hanging out with them because they were or seemed to be a bad influence. I resisted the idea and his demand to stop hanging out with them but eventually I agreed to save my mom the headache from his complaints. I thought okay, at least I can still hangout with my school friends and go to the community center. Not too long after he started to disapprove of virtually everything I wanted to do. He didn't like my choice of clothes because they weren't appropriate and he didn't want me to use the house phone for more than a few minutes. Eventually I couldn't use the phone at all. It reached a point where Natale literally tried to prevent me from leaving the apartment.

I argued with him about those things every time and complained to my mom about how unfair he was. I told her I couldn't understand why he was being that way but I wasn't going to leave it unchallenged. Our relationship became so toxic I just stopped talking to him all together. I hated living in the same house with him and I remember one day I got so upset with him I almost broke the apartment door down. The reason, you ask? The reason was my stepdad thought it was a great idea to place a lock on the door to keep me from leaving the house. Yes, he literally locked us all in the apartment with a padlock because I refused to comply with his demands to stay in and not leave the apartment.

In retrospect, I can't help but almost laugh about it because it all sounds pretty crazy, like scenes out of a wild movie. No one expects to see or experience similar situations happening in real life but they did to me. The unfortunate reality is that incident was only one of many other occasions. I was talking to my mom recently and asked her to reflect on some of these crazy moments. I wanted her help with remembering some of the details that were fuzzy in my mind.

She recalled one incident from our first winter in 2000 I had somehow almost completely forgotten. She said, "Do you remember the time you went to the laundromat on Niagara Street and got stuck there until midnight?" I responded "No, when did that happen?" She went on to say, "It happened when we were still on Rhode Island Street, and we were still new to Buffalo. Natale dropped you off at the laundromat earlier that day and left you there. He was supposed to return in a few hours after you were done washing clothes and bring you back home." She continued, "He didn't come back to get you that day. He probably went to drink with his friends and forgot about you. I was worried sick that night wondering what happened to my son and whether you were okay or not."

I asked her, "Really that happened?" I was trying my best to remember but I just couldn't recall those events. At the same time I wasn't surprised because: A) something like that would happen and B) with my mom's impressive memory I knew it had to be true. My mom then said, "I was so worried and didn't know what to do. I didn't know who to call, or how to get a hold of Natale. All I could do at the time was just pray and hope you were okay. That day, you were at the laundromat until it closed around midnight." I once again responded, "Wow, I can't believe I don't remember that day." I chuckled a bit the way I normally do when I don't know what else to say or how to react. It's a habit I've developed over the years that helps me keep from getting emotional or flat-out breaking down sometimes especially when I'm talking with my mother.

Mom went on to say, "When the laundromat closed you were left sitting outside in the cold for an unknown amount of time, before this Sudanese man who just happened to drive by saw you sitting there. He stopped, picked you up, and brought back home to me. If not for that Sudanese man God knows what might have happened to you that night."

Hearing that story from my mom was pretty wild and she also spoke a bit about what happened the next day when Natale came home which reminded me of another similar situation during the same winter at another laundromat. Yes, I know it may seem a bit redundant, but we did not have a washer and dryer at home and one of my regular chores during those days was laundry.

I was responsible for running many errands because my mother had my young siblings to care for, and because my stepdad did not take care of anything in the house. It wasn't regarded as his responsibility to complete many household chores. Coming from a traditionalist society and culture that often paints a man's duty as being the breadwinner, a provider and not much more my stepdad lived up to that image. Similar to most Sudanese men back home and abroad he embodied that ideal and did not venture much past that definition. Similar to most firstborn children in Sudanese society particularly boys, I had to fill that void to help my mother and the family.

The second winter laundromat incident occurred in November or December of 2000. I remember the experience vividly because there was plenty of snow on the ground and it was also my first encounter with law enforcement. The laundromat was located roughly ten or eleven city blocks from the house. I honestly can't explain why anyone thought it was a good idea to suggest that location when there were others much closer, but I went anyway because I didn't know better at the time.

I was dropped off at the laundromat with a few bags full of clothes but I had to figure out a way to get back home afterwards. The neighbor who dropped me off was not available to pick me back up, and I needed to get back before it was dark. I didn't have a shopping cart to load the bags on to push it all the way home, something I had done on multiple occasions. It would have also been a little tough given the snow accumulation on the ground but nonetheless it would have been helpful. My only option was to neatly fold all the clothes and tightly fit them into just two of those big black plastics trash bags so I could carry them one in each hand.

When I stepped out of the laundromat, the evening was cold, gray and the snow had started falling again. Carrying two trash bags full of clothes was a struggle from the moment I started walking home. For the first few blocks I felt a bit confident about making it home and only had to gently drop the bags a few times to take a quick break. However, the more I kept walking, the heavier the bags became, and the colder I started to feel all over especially in my toes and fingers.

I learned my lesson about the importance of wearing gloves in Buffalo so I made sure to have a pair this time around which was helpful, but I still didn't trust being out in the snow for long periods of time. I knew it was possible for things to play out differently if I didn't get home as soon as possible. Having already managed to survive my first frostbite experience just weeks before, I did not want to experience another.

Three-and-a-half blocks or so from the laundromat, I took my third or fourth minibreak and tried to warm up my fingers a bit before picking up the bag again. As I stood there for a second, I heard a vehicle slowly creeping up behind me. I happened to be standing not on the sidewalk but on the street close to the sidewalk. The sidewalks were not shoveled and were full of snow so I opted to walk on the side of the road where there was less snow. It was easier to carry the bags that way, and I could cover more ground and make it home a little faster. When I first saw the police car, I was actually happy because I figured they would ask where I was going and offer to help.

The officer in the driver seat rolled down his window and asked what I was doing and where I was going. I explained to him I was coming from the laundromat and heading home. He glanced at me and the two big black trash bags I was carrying, and said "Okay be careful." I waited a second wondering if he would ask where home was and offer to take me there. Instead, he started rolling up his window and before he could drive off, I asked, "Can you drop me home? It's down the street." He looked at me and flat out said, "No, I can't do that" then drove off.

I stood there for a second looking kind of shocked and confused. I wondered why the cop declined to help me? Isn't that what officers do? I picked up the trash bags and proceeded walking toward the house. Along the way I kept thinking how strange it was for these two officers to decline helping me even though I was clearly in need of help.

I thought about how helping people was the right thing to do and how in Egypt and back home in Sudan, people helped each other out all the time. I thought back to moments when I helped someone out, or when others offered to help me without asking. It was customary to offer help even if someone didn't ask for it. It's like when someone visits your home while you're enjoying a meal and you invite them to join. It was the right thing to do or so I thought.

I couldn't wrap my mind around what happened and it bothered me as I continued to walk home. However, I couldn't focus all my energy on trying to figure it out. I needed to try making it home as soon as possible before my hands and feet fell off from the cold. It took another thirty minutes or so after my encounter with the officers before I got home. As cold as it was outside, I managed to almost forget entirely about the weather because I was consumed with trying to figure out what just happened. I was trying to understand why those polices officers left me standing on the side of the road.

I was completely ignorant of the nature of policing in America, particularly with respect to race and the Black community. But there I was, a young *Cøllø*, South Sudanese and African boy, trying to understand something I had no idea about, but millions of people experience regularly in this country. I didn't understand why those officers stopped to ask me questions but did not offer help. I didn't understand in their eyes I probably fit the classification as just another Black or African American kid. In a society that views people with melanin-rich complexions with suspicion and more often than not as a threat, I didn't understand to them my true identity, culture, and rich history can probably be reduced to a simple idea such as the color of my skin.

It took a while and other encounters with police before I learned much more about the Black American experience with law enforcement in this country, which I was now automatically a part of as a result of my skin color.

In early 2003, we moved once again to our third home in Buffalo. This time the new house seemed to be much further away and in a completely different neighborhood. It was still in Buffalo's westside, and about seven or eight city blocks from our last apartment. I was in the eighth grade at that point and School 45 was much further away. The community center was no longer across the street and not really within walking distance from this location.

My siblings and I now had to wake up much earlier to prepare for school in time to catch the school bus every morning. Before we moved, I didn't mind missing the school bus and sometimes even missed it on purpose so I could walk to school with my friends. It was no big deal because the school was about a mile-and-a-half from home. That wasn't the case anymore and now whenever we missed the bus, Natale had to drop us off. He did not like that and honestly, I didn't either. So I made sure to catch the bus on time every morning and during the rare days when I did miss it, I preferred to stay home from school rather than ask for a ride. But I would swallow my pride and always ask so my siblings didn't have to miss school as well.

Fortunately, that nightmarish scenario didn't last long before was time to start high school. The summer before I started high school, I made new friends in our new neighborhood which was great because I knew some of them already from middle school. Some were in the eighth grade with me and others were literally my next-door-neighbors. I started hanging out with them often and I remember spending lots of time playing pick-up American football games.

CHAPTER 16

High School

I started high school in 2003 and attended Grover Cleveland High School. It was located less than a block away from our house and within a few minutes walking distance. My entire high school experience was interesting on so many levels. It was a time for many firsts which meant on my first day I had my first chance to make a good first impression on both my teachers and my classmates.

It was both exciting and a little nerve-racking to encounter and be surrounded by so many different personalities and attitudes my age as a freshman in high school. It was the first time I happened to be under the same roof with hundreds of teens who were not always on their best behavior. It was a time many students got a glimpse of who they are or at least who their classmates think you are. If they weren't careful, whatever distorted image their peers painted of them could end up sticking with them for the next four years. For most teenagers, high school was the ultimate social experiment.

My high school experience could best be described as a true learning experience. I don't mean in the traditional sense in reference to academic excellence or in reference to "how I became an ideal student-athlete." It was a true learning experience in the sense I went through a major phase of personal growth and learned a lot about myself as well as the people around me. In addition to my academics I learned to be more self-reliant and to take care of myself, I discovered true friendships, and toward the end of my high school career I started to focus more on my future.

My first day of high school was filled with excitement more than anything else, but I wasn't sure what to expect. My homeroom was filled with a decent amount of incoming freshman totaling about twenty students or more. It was a diverse group of students a quite familiar sight coming from International School 45. While waiting for our new homeroom teacher to show up, I started a random conversation with some of my new classmates. Among them was a very down-to-earth cool kid whom I considered to be one of my good friends throughout high school.

Within the first few months, I think most high school kids have an idea as to where they fit in, if at all. You're either with the cool kids—usually the student athletes, the pretty boys and girls and those popular by association—or you're with everyone else. At Grover, it was sometimes hard to figure out who was who because there were so many different groups. The majority of the student body at the time was African American followed by Spanish-speaking students who were mostly Puerto Ricans, and the rest were a diverse group of kids from all over. There was a sizable number of immigrant and refugee students from different countries and backgrounds and that sums up the layout of the land at Grover Cleveland High School.

Many students only associated with and hung out with other students from their respective group. It was interesting trying to figure out how high school works compared to middle school and how to navigate through it but eventually we all learn there is no silver bullet for it. I always considered myself to be a friendly kid who was willing to get along with just about anyone and that's how I carried myself. If you were cool and treated me with respect, I was cool and happy to reciprocate. I tried my best to get along with everyone. I figured it was the best thing to do. It didn't matter to me whether you consider yourself the most popular kid in school or not. If you were cool with me, I was cool with you.

Grey zone or neutral zone would be an accurate description of the space I was in throughout high school. I didn't mind associating with classmates from across the popularity spectrum and grade levels. I knew some popular kids and I knew others who weren't so popular, but regardless I considered people from both groups my friends. It didn't matter what other students thought about me or the students I associated with as far as I was concerned it was irrelevant. I also didn't try to forcefully fit in with any one group or another. I just tried to go with the flow a phrase my best friend in high school, Jimy, used to say often. I never wanted to come across as fake or disingenuous to anyone, to my teachers or to any student.

The grey zone wasn't always a great space to be in and trying to get along with everyone didn't always work to my advantage. There were times when some students saw it as an opportunity to target me for jokes about being an African student. It was often African American students making these jokes which was a bit ironic because we were all considered Black. Those moments usually started with off-color and unpleasant jokes about African stereotypes and my dark complexion. The first time it happened I didn't make a big deal of it because I knew some of the students liked to mess with underclassmen as an easy way to get some laughs. I also didn't want to be a part of a disturbance by arguing with a student trying his best to be a class clown.

Taking the high road and being the bigger better person did not work well in high school. Before long, I learned being silent was probably worse than being part of the chaos. Perhaps not for the teachers and staff who had to deal with it, but it was worse for me. Some students started to make it nearly impossible to sit in class without starting a problem and I made sure to respond in kind. I didn't want to be disruptive or get caught in heated arguments in the middle of class, but I was unwilling to back down and let someone take advantage of or humiliate me. I knew if I were to let it go on unchecked, they would try to paint a huge target on my back and I wasn't going to let that happen.

One strange fact about high school is the same kids who might try to make your experience hell might also try to become your friends or "frienemies" (friend and enemy). That was certainly my experience. Some of the students who tried targeting me with their lame jokes at first, later became kind of cool with me. Part of the reason was I had a pretty smart mouth and didn't hold back whenever anyone tried to bully me. Some of the kids who tried to get a laugh by cracking jokes about me ended up being the laughingstock on many occasions. But I never held a grudge against them or against anyone else. As far as I was concerned if you were willing to move past whatever situation occurred between us, I was willing to do the same.

Outside of school things were very different, and I was only around a certain group of friends. Most of my in-school friends lived in different parts of town. Some of them lived in the eastside of town which was predominantly Black and others lived in different areas far from school. Going to hang out with them outside of school often required public transportation. The guys I hung out with outside of school were all Sudanese. There were a few different reasons for that. First, we all lived relatively close to one another, and second, we all grew up together and were more comfortable around each other. We had an established routine that kept all of us together throughout our high school years. Some of the guys were a class or two ahead of me, and some were in the same grade with me. We all basically had the same interests, which mostly centered around figuring out ways to buy new clothes and shoes for school, playing sports, and having fun.

I couldn't and didn't want to ask my stepdad for money to buy anything, and my mother wasn't working during those years, so I had to figure out a way to make my own money. I knew there were ways to scrape up a few dollars here and there to buy a decent pair of sneakers which was a must for every high school student. It was just a necessity if you wanted to be respected and not picked on. I figured I already had some work experience from the winter before I started high school, so I could manage to find something similar to make money.

One of my friends from the old neighborhood and I went shoveling snow that winter and earned $30 each from clearing a few driveways. It only took a few hours and felt good despite the freezing cold. I only needed to find a gig that would multiply that amount by three and allow me to earn $90. That would've been enough to buy a pair of white Nike Air Force Ones. Along with Air Jordon's, those sneakers were a must-have in high school and I wanted the high-top Ones but I was willing to settle for the low-tops to start and work my way up. I figured those ones could last a few months if

I took good care of them, at least until I could earn enough to buy another new pair. The issue I was left to grapple with was finding a gig that fall since winter was months away and I needed money now.

That fall was tough because I didn't find a gig to earn money, but my sophomore year was much better. I managed to start my first job during the summer and I can remember how excited I was about it. The idea of having a job and the potential to earn my own money was awesome. I thought, *Finally, I'm going to be able to buy whatever I want* and I couldn't wait for my first check. The other reason I was happy about the job was because a few of my friends were also employees there and we were now coworkers. They were like my brothers and we practically did everything together so it was a plus that we also work together.

My first job was at a church located on the eastside of Buffalo and I was a part of the maintenance crew. My friend Steve was the first youth employee amongst us working at St. Martin's, and then my best friend Jimy joined before I was added to the mix. For a while before I was hired, I basically lobbied Steve, Jimy, and *Abuna* to bring me on board at least to help out occasionally even if it was just for a few hours a week.

Abuna is an Arabic word for Father and it is the title we all used to refer to Father Ron in the Sudanese community. Reverend Father Ron was the pastor at St. Martin de Porres Roman Catholic Church at the time, and also our employer. Before I started working for St. Martin's, I knew of *Abuna* and I was already familiar with his reputation throughout the Sudanese community. He had developed a great reputation for working with Sudanese and refugee families from many other communities in Buffalo. One of the Sudanese families

Abuna was close with was Mut's and Dew's families, two of my oldest friends from Buffalo. I remember one of the first times seeing *Abuna* was at the pizza party at Mut's house a few years back.

There were a few other different occasions I recall meeting *Abuna*. In fact my family and I once met him at his old parish. Before he was named pastor at St. Martin's, Father Ron was associate pastor at St. Bernadette's in Orchard Park a suburb of Buffalo. We were there for a Christmas party along with Mut's and a few other Sudanese families. That year I also met Mrs. Joan for the first time.

Mrs. Joan worked with *Abuna* at St. Bernadette's and later at St. Martin's as the pastoral associate for many years. She was also heavily involved in working with the Sudanese and refugee communities for as long as I've known her and her family. Through their work at St. Martin De Porres, (ROTA) Reaching Out 2 Africa, and so many other areas in the community, Father Ron and Mrs. Joan have made a huge difference over the years. [17] Their impact reached not only the Sudanese and refugee communities they've dedicated so much time and energy, but reached my family and my life personally.

FAITH

In the South Sudanese community the church has a central role in family life. For many South Sudanese, the first thing they look for regardless of where they are in this world is the nearest church. We are taught at a young age faith in God lights our paths and we must never stray from our faith no matter what happens in this life. The church is always there

---

17   "A Brief History of ROTA," Reach Out 2 Africa, Accessed March 5, 2021.

to help guide us through all challenges and God will not abandon us no matter how hopeless things may seem. For a community of people who have been through decades of civil war and have experienced unbelievable challenges, faith in God is often the only thing keeping most of us moving forward.

Growing up in Khartoum, attending church was a regular but important part of everyday life. As a child I didn't yet understand much about Christianity but as I grew older, I started to learn the importance of the Christian faith. At the age of ten in Egypt I chose to be baptized and accepted the name Emmanuel as my Christian name. My belief in God and my Catholic faith has always guided me in the right direction and served me well. Without it, I can't say for certain if I could have found within me the strength needed to keeping pushing through some of the most difficult times in my life.

People often say "God works in mysterious ways" and I believe that to be true especially with regards to the people God places in our lives. Another popular phrase is "everything happens for a reason." That phrase is also true, and the perfect place where those two phrases proved to be true simultaneously was St. Martin De Porres Roman Catholic Church. The mystery can be said to be my church family and all the amazing people who came into my life through St. Martin's. The reasons were to build up and help me become the best possible version of my former self.

At St. Martin's, Sunday mass was always lively and I enjoyed the experience every week. The church was always full of people singing and praising the Lord and our gospel choir was unbelievably amazing. Considered the only Black Catholic church in the diocese of Buffalo, St. Martin's was unique at every level. It didn't feel like a typical Roman Catholic church it felt more like a Southern Baptist church somewhere in the middle of Georgia or Alabama. The congregation regularly joined the choir in singing and praising the Lord with so much passion, if a stranger walked into the church, they would have a hard time believing we were a Catholic Church.

Abuna always did an excellent job connecting the gospel and its teaching to everyday life and presented it in his own unique way. Young or old, the message seemed to resonate with us all more often than not and it was powerful. At St. Martin's, there was always so much going on around you that uplifted your spirit, leaving a true sense of faith that could be felt by anyone walking through the church doors. That sense of community often reminded me of *Sakakini* back in Cairo, which I had not realized I'd missed until that point.

After mass on Sundays, Steve, Jimy, and I normally gathered at church and brainstormed plans for the upcoming week. Around the same time *Abuna*, Mrs. Joan, or Danny— our maintenance supervisor— would often give us an idea of our work schedule for the week. Jimy and I started to be become closer friends during that first year working together partly because our schedules often overlapped and also because we were around each other outside of work. We went to Grover together, played sports and went to the same after school community center.

When we first met, I was a freshman and he was a sophomore, and since I was new to the school, I tried making friends with people I had things in common with like sports. At Grover, I was interested in joining the soccer team. Jimy was already on the team along with Sabit and Jor, two of my other Sudanese friends. I was eager to join the team when

I discovered the school once had two teams—junior varsity and varsity. That year however, the JV team was eliminated and both teams were merged into one varsity team. That was great and exciting news because it meant I had a chance to play soccer at the highest high school level as a freshman. I didn't have to wait a year or two or work my way up from junior varsity to varsity as a freshman.

Outside of school, work, and the soccer field, we spent most of our time at the youth center at Holy Cross Church. The community center was located in the basement of the church and it was a good place to go for help with homework. The center had a game room and basketball gym available for use after completing our schoolwork. Throughout high school we spent countless hours at Holy Cross and it became our go-to spot every day after school. It was really a great, fun, and safe place for us to be, and the level of competition on the basketball court just made it that much more fun.

Our group was pretty tight-knit. Jimy, Akin, Jor, Steve and I were the core group of friends who were always together. At school we often saw one another in passing at the gym, or at lunch if our schedules happened to coincide. However, we always met after school at Holy Cross and then at the Mariner Homes just a few blocks down the street from the church. During those early days none of us had a driver's license yet or access to a car. Whenever we needed a ride somewhere far outside the neighborhood, we relied on Abuna occasionally to pick us up, drop us off, or at times both. Steve was the point person for that task because he was the senior employee at St. Martin's and we trusted him to get the job done.

More often than not *Abuna* would always show up for us in his metallic gray Dodge Caravan. Every Friday evening after school, all five of us looked forward to going skating at

Rainbow Rink in North Tonawanda just north of the city of Buffalo in Niagara country. After a few hours of hanging out at the rink, Steve would call Abuna and he would graciously show up to drop off each of us at home.

The rest of the week we walked everywhere by foot. Akin, Steve, and Jor all lived at Mariner Homes also known as the Homes. Jimy and I did not. Steve is Jor's older brother and Akin's friend; I've known them for almost as many years as Oscar and Mut. I knew all of them before we became friends in high school but we didn't attend the same middle school. Right after the community center closed around 8:00 p.m. or so during school nights, we often walked to the Homes to hang out for another hour or two before going our separate ways.

We spent countless hours sitting around the Homes talking about every topic you can imagine. We played pick-up American football in the parking lot and occasionally ventured across the highway to LaSalle Park. Jimy and I always walked home together from the Homes. The housing complex is located near downtown Buffalo and Jimy lived on Grant street which is quite a distance to cover walking. I lived near our high school which was approximately halfway to Grant street and roughly a thirty-minute walk from the Homes.

From my house to Jimy's house on Grant was approximately another thirty minutes. We had a routine for this hour-long walk. First, we walked together from the homes to my house then from my house till about the halfway point to Jimy's house. At that point each of us walked the rest of the way home on our own. During those days nothing was off topic between Jimy and I it was like a therapy session. We talked and laughed about everything but mostly girls.

When Akin got his learner's permit and started driving his dad's minivan it was a game changer. We all now had access to transportation by default and no longer had to rely on Abuna as much for our Friday night plans. We went everywhere with that van. It was a dark purple-colored van and it was recognizable around the neighborhood. Every weekend we had two things to look forward to: skating on Fridays and church on Sunday mornings.

However, there was a catch. To join on Friday nights, you had to pray Akin got the van from his dad, and everyone had to have gas money to ride in the van. Fortunately Akin who we also called Hakeem was able to secure the van nine out of ten times. But there were no guarantees for anyone without a dollar or two to chip in for gas because they were more likely to stay home. The only other thing each and every one of us needed to make sure we had a good time was $5 for a brand-new white tee shirt, and $5 for entrance fee at the rink

Thinking back to those days reminds me of all the good times with my boys. I didn't realize how much of a blessing they were in my life. We didn't quite realize it at the time but we protected each other in more ways than one. First of all our friendship was truly more of a brotherhood. We looked out for one another at all times and kept each other from doing a lot of stupid and regrettable things. Second, we all shared similar interests. We just wanted to have fun with a good group of our friends.

During those high school years we rarely hung out with anyone outside of our immediate group. All of our lives consisted of going to school, working after school, and going to the community center at Holy Cross during the week. During the weekend it was Friday nights at the rink or other teen night events, LaSalle Park on Saturdays to play soccer, and Sunday mass to end or start the week.

The rest of the time we had to ourselves were spent at home or taking care of our household responsibilities for our families. Akin, Jimy, and I were the oldest children in each household and that came with its own pressures and expectations. The schedules we all maintained helped make things a little easier and kept us out of trouble. It's also worth noting none of us had much interest in getting involved or caught up with the wrong people and avoided situations that could have encouraged it.

We made sure to help keep each other stay away from gang activity, drugs, and from getting caught up in the system. We were able to do so because each and every one of us knew it would be unacceptable to get involved in some of these activities. If any of us did, it would reflect poorly on all of us and it would be considered an embarrassment to our families in the eyes of the community. We were old enough to understand family reputation is important and can easily be tarnished by any risky or irresponsible behavior. None of us wanted to be the one who brought shame to our parents or to our group of friends and their families.

The other part of that equation was simply the fact in high school none of the guys were really interested in experimenting with certain risky behavior. In Sudan, alcohol was illegal and considered taboo in Khartoum where most of us were born. People who consumed it were often ostracized. It was frowned upon in the community to consume alcohol and that was still our perception at that age. The idea of experimenting with anything else such as weed (marijuana) or *bongo* in Arabic was like jumping out the window of a moving train. It was considered be throwing your life away so there was no room for error in the community.

Lastly, I think we were lucky to all have migrated to this country at the age we all did. We were old enough to remember some things and important lessons from back home that helped guide us away from trouble. Most of it was driven by fear of what might happened if we did in fact get into trouble, but some of it was simply out of ignorance or lack of interest. In high school we still had limited exposure to certain aspects of American life and culture. Much of it was not yet normalized in our community and we had to always proceed with caution. This was a blessing and helped guide all of us through that pivotal point in our young lives.

CHAPTER 17

The College Process

———

I started my college career at the local community college in the fall of 2007. Before attending Erie Community College (ECC) I didn't quite know what I wanted to do after graduating high school. I honestly did not seriously begin to think about my next move after high school until just months before graduation. During my junior and senior years I had a few meetings with my guidance counselor about college and the application processes but not much more. The idea of going to college seemed a little farfetched, and I kept telling myself I still had plenty of time to prepare and make a decision. I kept thinking in that way until it was almost too late to attend college that year.

My senior year was mostly focused on trying to have fun and graduating. Like most high school seniors, the main idea was to make sure high school ended on a memorable note. That's exactly what I wanted to do. I wanted to simply hang out with my friends and have a good time, in and out of school, and enjoy the perks of being a senior. I also knew to graduate with my class and walk across the stage, I had to make sure I passed my required classes. I knew I was capable of passing without being an honor roll student, which was fine by me.

There were a few different reasons I adopted that attitude and I didn't realize the negative repercussions it may have on my academic future at least not until I started college. The first reason was besides my teachers, I was the only one who looked at my report cards. Reason number two was I felt hardly any pressure at home about my academic performance and I thought I was doing just fine. Reason number three: I basically knew nothing about the reality of college and life after high school.

With regards to the first reason it wasn't that my parents didn't care about my grades or my mother didn't bother to ask about them, it was simply expected of me to do well at school. I can't speak for my stepdad, but I understood my mother had expectations. Those expectations were supposed to be enough to help motivate and keep me on the right track in school. Strangely enough they sort of did, but only to a certain extent.

What my mom expected of me was to be a good student and get good grades because I was old enough to understand the value of education. In actuality, I was only pushing myself hard enough to make it past the finish line in high school. During moments when I felt a lack of motivation to keep going or focus on my education, I had to remember what my mother expected, which was that I take responsibility for my education.

In addition to this, I had to always keep in mind I was also responsible for setting a good example for my siblings. No matter what I decided to do with my life, I always felt obligated to think about the example I was setting for my brothers and sisters. If any of them were to decide to follow in my footsteps or pave their own path I knew the best possible way to do so would be through their education. I never lost sight of that and held on to it, and often reflected on my obligation to them as one of the main factors that helped push me to complete my education at every level.

Reason number two was similar to many immigrant and refugee families my parents were faced with many challenges as newcomers to this country. Learning the English language was one of those challenges and language is major factor that touches every aspect of life. My mom depended on my siblings and me to help translate and respond to report cards and letters sent from school.

I had been doing so since the sixth grade, explaining permission slips and reviewing everyone else's report cards and over the years I'd grown accustomed to it. It was fine by me and I felt more comfortable with the way things were in Buffalo having survived through the struggle in Egypt. I figured as long as I did fairly well at school I was off the hook and didn't have to worry about any added pressure from my mother.

Reason number three was the toughest to deal with. My limited exposure and lack of knowledge about the college process had real-life damaging consequences staring me right in the face. It was a reality check against the phrase "what you don't know, can't hurt you." A common phrase people like to throw around to make themselves or others feel better about certain situations. I've heard it on more than one occasion and it's silly because it's not true. Sometimes what you don't know can and will hurt you. The best thing to do about it is to education yourself and find a way to solve the problem at hand—a tough lesson I had to learn the hard way to start my college career.

The idea of college was clear to me and always had been. All my life I knew it was important to attend college. The challenge however, was more about the how which proved to be more complicated than I thought. I had a lot of unanswered questions at the start of the process. *What school or schools were in the Buffalo area? What could they offer me? When could I apply? What was the application process? What did I need for it? Who could I talk with about these questions?* I had so many questions and didn't know where or whom to turn to. I couldn't ask my mom about it, and my stepdad and I weren't on speaking terms anymore because we had a deteriorated relationship by that point.

We had access to guidance counselors at school, but I remember discussing college only a few times with a guidance counselor before my senior year and graduation. I needed additional guidance to help with understanding not only the importance of my decision but the entire processes. Our counselors had many students to deal with so naturally they only had a limited time to advise each student. The times I spoke with my counselor, she discussed basic topics like application deadlines and degree programs for a few of the local colleges. I had no idea what questions to ask during those meetings and so I listened to her instructions and advice instead.

By the time I was prepared to walk the stage during graduation I had successfully completed a total of one application for Buffalo State College. The application process was not an easy one and I struggled to gather all information and necessary documents to complete it. I felt there was no one to rely on or assist me through this transitional phase in my life and at times I felt completely lost.

I wanted to consider other schools outside of western New York but I could not. We had college recruiters from New York City show up to Grover and talk with us about NYC schools. They talked about academic and sports programs I was interested in but my mother was opposed to the idea of going to college outside of Buffalo. I knew my best bet was to focus on getting into a local college and then figure it out as I went. A few weeks after sending in my application to Buffalo State I received a letter from their admissions office. I was a little nervous about it but excited to discover what it said.

After reading through the letter, I realized it was a rejection and not an acceptance letter which was disappointing. By then I didn't have much time to start thinking about my next move. My options were limited because Buffalo State was the only school I applied to. I did not apply to the University of Buffalo (UB), Canisius, D'youville, Daemen, Medaille, or any of the other four-year universities or colleges in and around Buffalo. It wasn't because I didn't want to apply; it was simply because I didn't know much about those schools or their application processes. I felt completely overwhelmed on occasion trying to research and learn about the different process at times I felt hopeless.

When I thought about the large schools like the University at Buffalo (UB), I imagined them to be such a big deal and thought only certain people were qualified to attend. I didn't think of myself as having what it takes to attend such a school. It's difficult to explain my thoughts and perceptions about some of these institutions at the time, but it was almost debilitating. I felt more lost at that point than at any other time in my life. I even wanted to call it quits and just give up on the idea of attending college that year.

Giving up wasn't an option and no matter what happened, I still had to try to get into college before the fall semester and figure out the rest later. I still had time to apply to Erie Community College (ECC) which some of my senior classmates had already applied to. I also knew a few students from different high schools who had attended ECC in the past for a year or two then transferred to four-year schools. A few others were in the process of transferring to Buffalo State, UB, or to one of the other four-year schools in the area. I was able to speak with a couple of them about ECC and those conversations proved to be helpful in convincing me to apply rather than stay home for a full year after high school.

I can't say I was initially thrilled about it but I'm glad my first college experience happened to be at a community college. I didn't appreciate that until later on in my college career. During my first year at ECC I was very much reserved and mostly kept to myself. On campus, my interactions were limited and I only associated with friends and people I knew. I wasn't very social and I wasn't comfortable venturing outside of my comfort zone.

Attending ECC did not appear to be very different from high school even though I was no longer there. It certainly was different but felt slightly familiar in a few ways. First, there was a diverse student body often roaming across the atrium of the former downtown Buffalo post office building. At any given moment, you're likely to see a mix of young high school graduates and older working professionals passing by. Some were there studying for a two-year associate degree and others were there working on transferring to earn a bachelor's degree at a four-year college or university.

I was amongst the new students fresh out of high school looking to earn an associate degree and searching for a career path. I decided to pursue criminal justice as my degree program, and I did so for a few reasons. First, it came across as the most interesting program offered. Second, I had no interest in healthcare-related programs, information technology

(IT), or any of the other programs offered at ECC. Criminal justice felt more interesting because of the subject matter and the career options it offered.

With a criminal justice degree I had the option to become a law enforcement officer which was exciting. During my first semester I took two courses that helped make up my mind: Introduction to Criminal Justice and sociology. Intro to criminal justice was really interesting and ignited my fascination with studying and understanding law. Sociology challenged my thoughts, beliefs, and preconceptions about society. It opened my mind in so many ways and sparked my interest in politics and the world around me.

For the first time in my life I started thinking in depth about important issues and topics impacting my daily life. Both professors in those two courses were excellent educators and they pushed students to break out of their comfort zones and engage. There were other courses I found intriguing, but not at the same level. I enjoyed the lectures and discussions in class every week especially regarding the nature of the American judicial system. I remember at one point I became so interested in learning about New York State criminal law I started to carry around the New York State Penal Law Code.

My second year at ECC was a bit more complicated. I was content with criminal justice as my degree program, and my academics looked good and on track. The plan was to complete my associate degree that year and attend the police academy the following year. After graduating from academy, I would begin my career as a law enforcement officer with the Buffalo Police Department (BPD). While serving the community as an officer, I planned on pursuing a bachelor's degree (BA) in political science and then get a law degree.

I happen to also join the Erie Community College men's soccer team in the fall of 2008. That year my schedule was jam-packed and split between the three ECC campuses. I attended courses at the city campus in downtown Buffalo and the north campus in Williamsville a suburb east of the city. Soccer training and home games were at the south campus in the town of Orchard Park south of the city. I did not own a vehicle at the time and relied on public transportation to get around to all three campus.

For courses at North Campus I had to take the metro from downtown to University Station which is the last station on the line. Then, I had to get on a bus for a lengthy ride to reach campus two to three times a week. For soccer training at South Campus, I had to take a forty-five-minute to an hour-long bus ride from downtown Buffalo. It wasn't all bad because I napped on the bus for most of the ride every time.

I was exhausted from my school schedule but I still had other responsibilities outside of it. I was an AmeriCorps volunteer at Father Belle Community Center and I still had to help out with lots of things at home. Adjusting was a bit difficult at first, but I didn't have a choice and quickly learned to normalize and deal with it all because I knew it wasn't going to be easy. I didn't expect school to be easy and I just had to accept it as one more challenge life presented.

I've never been a stranger to tough times and I'd grown used to dealing with my share of challenges which is why I struggled to understand how I ended up where I was during my third semester at ECC. Not much had changed in my life during the spring semester I was dealing with some family issues but it wasn't anything I couldn't handle. My stepdad and I were butting heads like we have in the past, but for some reason I was feeling overburdened by it and couldn't shake it off like usual.

I was thinking about the problems he and I had often and I even began to wonder about my father. It was strange because I hadn't thought about him in a long time. I've had moments when I wondered about him, my father, and about how he may be doing back home in Sudan or wherever he was. However, those moments were few and far between. When I did wonder about him, I also thought about the rest of my extended family.

This time was different. I thought about him often and raised questions about our relationship or lack thereof. I thought about the fact he and I had not spoken in nearly a decade since I left Khartoum in 1999. I wondered why. I thought about how it was more than likely he had married and started a new family. I wondered if I now had little brothers and sisters from him in Sudan whom I knew nothing about. I had so many questions with no answers and no one to ask but my mother. I knew this was a sensitive topic for her and I wondered if it was wise to even ask.

I was conflicted. I didn't know whether it would be appropriate to ask or not. So I opted to keep it to myself instead and tried to get past this inquisitive phase on my own. While I was struggling in silence to push past this moment of identity crisis, my stepfather Natale and I were having a very difficult time getting along. For some reason he wanted to reinstate some sort of control over my life, and I was completely opposed to that in every way, shape, and form.

I was old enough, mature enough, and responsible enough to be left to my own devices, and I didn't need him for anything in my life. I felt he never really played a significant role in my life up until that point—especially since we moved to Buffalo—and he shouldn't try to get involved any more. I was convinced the only thing he was interested in was trying to destroy my life and I wasn't going to allow it. I was justified in being defiant and rebelling against him and I had every right to protect myself from him. As the oldest in the family, I felt obligated to protect the entire family from him especially my mom.

I lived in the upstairs apartment of our duplex house with my brother Aken at the time. My mother convinced me to stay home instead of moving out with some friends and offered a pretty sweet deal. I initially planned on moving to campus at the earliest opportunity to whatever college I got into for the full college experience, but I also wanted to get away from home. I thought living in a dorm room at any of the local colleges would've been my best bet. That plan fell through when I didn't get into Buffalo State.

I didn't have any other options either because I did not apply anywhere else. The next best thing was to move upstairs into the vacant unit, if I was willing to make it happen. I wanted to leave the house and move completely into my own space. I wanted to be free from the drama at home. I wanted to live my college years the way I saw fit.

The offer my mother presented was this: I could live in the second-floor apartment free of rent for however long if I was willing to take responsibility for my utility bills and renovating the unit. As much as I wanted to be on my own, I knew better than to turn down such a great offer. I jumped at the opportunity and immediately agreed to the terms. I didn't care much for taking on any more bills because I thought my phone bill was enough but I also didn't want to pass on the chance to have my own apartment rent free.

The two-bedroom apartment unit was in good shape and only needed minor renovations. My aunt and her family lived in it just the year before and they only moved out after buying a home of their own. I was excited about having my own place so I decided to get to work right away. First, I started to figure out what needed to be done and how to get it done. Second, I started working as hard as I could to complete the project and push up the move in date. That decision turned out to be an excellent decision because it ended up making such a huge difference in my life in so many ways.

POLICE ACADEMY

As I was preparing to complete my degree program at ECC, I started looking into the application process for the police academy. The academy was located at north Campus the same campus I attended most of most of my courses at the time which made things easier. In the Spring of 2010, I started the registration process for the academy and completed the physical evaluation with flying colors. That boosted my confidence and felt like a great way to begin laying down the groundwork for a career in law enforcement. I was at the beginning of my path to becoming the first Sudanese American to join the Buffalo Police Department.

It was an exciting moment and I was looking forward to my first day the academy. All I needed to do next was register for the courses. After I passed the physical evaluation, I went to the registration office and requested a form. As I began to fill out the form the registrar asked a few confirmation questions one of which was about my citizenship. She asked "Are you a US citizen?" to which I replied "No, I'm not." She looked at me as if it was not big deal and replied "Oh, you have to be a US citizen to register for the police academy."

This was shocking news to me. Suddenly, I was left standing there with the registration form in my hands trying to figure out what just happened. With a puzzled look on my face, I asked "You do?" and she confirmed once again "Yea, you do." At that moment I set down the unfinished form with my name on it and the few personal details I managed to write down and walked out of the office. As I walked away, I thought, *Did that just happen?* I wondered *how is it I'm just now discovering this important detail? Why didn't anyone mention it when I asked about the application process weeks before?* I wasn't necessarily upset but very disappointed. I walked across campus from the main office building toward the student parking lot where my car was parked, a typical five- to seven-minute walk that felt so much further away this time around.

As I walked across campus, I was racking my brain with questions about US citizenship instead of the academy. *Why was I required to be a citizen for the academy? More importantly where do I go and who do I ask about the citizenship process? What did I need to become a citizen and how long did it take? Would I be granted citizenship in time to register for the academy next semester?* I had many other questions and figured I would need to make this a priority and do some research. So I did.

Fortunately, I had friends and knew some people in the Sudanese community who have successfully gone through the US naturalization process. They were now naturalized American citizens. My family and I had been permanent residents for over five years at the time and I had my green card which was step one in the naturalization process.

I made sure to do my own research in addition to gathering more information and fact-checking everything I'd heard from the new citizens in the community. Immediately after that I started my application process. While waiting for the process to take its course I thought about my next academic move now that the police academy was basically out of question. I needed to plan ahead in case I was not able to attend the academy the following academic year. I had to go back to the drawing board and alter my three-part career plan to make the necessary adjustments. I was still in part one of the plan which was to complete my associate degree and move on to part two which was completing the police academy and a bachelor's degree.

The plan for a bachelor's degree was to attend school on a part-time basis and complete the program at a four-year school over an extended period of time. During the three- to four-year period, I would work full-time as a police officer. Since US citizenship was a requirement for this plan to work, I had to change course and place the academy on hold until further notice.

CANISIUS COLLEGE

For my bachelor's, I decided to look at political science programs offered throughout western New York. I was now more familiar with the different colleges and universities in the area and I was confident I could find a good program for my BA. I was also interested in exploring the possibility of joining a men's soccer program as a transfer student with two years of eligibility. I managed to narrow my options down to two schools, both with great academic reputations and good soccer programs. The first was Canisius college and the second was (UB) University at Buffalo.

I decided to apply to Canisius College because it was one of the best schools in western New York, and it had a Division I soccer team. I thought if I got into Canisius I could try to secure a spot by proving I could be a valuable player for the team. I also thought maybe, just maybe if I was lucky enough, I could land at least a partial athletic scholarship. With a $30,000–$40,000 annual tuition, securing any amount through an athletic scholarship would go a long way to help cover the cost of attending Canisius.

I knew it was a long shot, and I was conscious of the fact I may not even be accepted to attend the school, but I was hopeful. By the grace of God I was accepted to Canisius. I remember how happy I was about it. Immediately, I called my mother and *Abuna* to share the great news. Through the phone, Mom and *Abuna* could probably hear my heightened level of excitement about it while they were trying to congratulate me.

I couldn't wait until the beginning of the fall semester so I could start attending the school. That summer, I spent months preparing and stayed on top of everything to ensure I had a smooth transfer process. I followed up regularly with ECC to make sure all my records were sent in on time, along with my transcripts financial aid documents, and the additional paperwork for programs I may be eligible for at Canisius.

One of those programs was the Educational Opportunity Program. It is a New York State program intended to support low-income and first-generation college students through their academic career. I wasn't aware of it, but I qualified for the program at ECC and discovered my eligibility for the program at Canisius College. That was great news, but first I had to figure out how to navigate the application process before I could access whatever funds were available. The rest of my tuition however, had to be paid through a combination of student and parent loans my mother had to take on.

Outside of academics, I spent half of my summer focused on intense training to improve my soccer skills. I felt confident in my ability to showcase my talent and potential for growth and improvement under the right coaching staff. I knew Canisius would be very different from ECC, and if I wanted a chance to play I had to showcase something very special. I also knew there were probably many other students who want to join the team just as much so I had to be well prepared.

Having played for the ECC men's soccer team, I knew there were areas and skill sets I needed to develop further. I was willing to work hard and improve them to compete at a higher level. At best I thought, I would make the team and possibly secure a partial athletic scholarship. At worst, I would not make the cut. Either way, I looked forward to tryouts and feedback about my soccer talents from the coaching staff.

During the summer, I reached out to the Canisius men's soccer team's head coach and asked about the tryout process. I made sure to reach out early enough so I had time to prepare myself and try to be in the best shape possible. I remember going to the athletic center for the first time and asking around for the head coach's office. Luckily, I found him behind his desk that day and he was kind enough to invite me in and answer some of my questions. After our brief conversation, I left feeling pretty good about my chances of making it through at least the first stage of tryouts.

He basically told me, like any other students interested in joining the team, I would have an opportunity to show off my skills during tryouts in a few weeks. I visited his office sometime in July and the season did not start until September. When I left his office, I didn't know the exact dates or times for tryouts, but he told me at the time they were working on scheduling. I figured that was normal and when I got home that afternoon, I followed up with an email asking to be updated on the dates and times once the schedule was out and thanked him for his time.

A couple of weeks went by and I didn't hear anything back from the coach so I followed up with another email asking for updates. Still, no clear answer on tryout dates, times, or locations. It was now late August, with just weeks before the start of the school year and the soccer season. I was a bit confused as to why tryouts hadn't happened by that point and what was going on. I guess I should've suspected or figured something was wrong but I trusted the coach and thought I should just wait for his direction.

When I set my mind on doing something, I can be relentless and persistent in trying to reach or accomplish that goal. My desire to join the Canisius college men's soccer team was one of those things I set my sights on, and I was willing to do everything I could for a chance to prove myself. I remember following up with the coach on another day and asking if he had decided on tryout dates. I didn't ask whether I could come tryout I asked when I could come tryout for the team before the season started. That's when he finally responded and sent an email with a date, time, and address.

It was scheduled for a week or so later after I received the email. I was excited and anticipated a full session most likely designed to test skill set, soccer IQ, and fitness along with many other factors required to play for a Division I team. I made sure to arrive at the tryout site about fifteen minutes early. To my surprise I ended up in front of a small, vacant plot of land in some residential neighborhood. It was a quarter to 5:00 p.m. on a cool, dark cloudy summer evening. I thought this couldn't be right. I started to wonder if the coach accidentally sent me the wrong address or if I missed something. I double-checked my email for the address and indeed it was correct.

I waited about ten to fifteen minutes to see if anyone else would show up, to see if any other player or coaching staff was running late. However, no one showed up—not the coach or any member of the coaching staff or any student athletes. That evening I waited by myself on standby confused and wondering why no one else was there, and why tryouts would be held in Amherst to begin with?

Amherst, New York is a suburban town just outside of Buffalo. It is one of the wealthiest areas in western New York and with a predominately white population. I didn't think anything suspicious about the tryout location being in Amherst because many students at Canisius came from affluent families. I thought maybe the school had ties to a nice park or soccer field in Amherst. Thinking back to that time, I should have probably asked why tryouts would be in a location twenty minutes away from Canisius when we have an artificial turf soccer field on premise?

The following morning I personally went to the coach's office and asked what happened the evening before. He looked directly at me and said, "There are only thirty spots on the roster and the program is full." He continued and said "We get players from Europe and I can't put everyone on the team." As he spoke, I was surprise by how nonchalant he was about everything he was saying to me. He spoke as if it was no big deal. He literally sent me to some random location in anticipation for trying out for the team, something he clearly never had the intention of letting me do.

Honestly, I couldn't quite understand what was happening, nor was I able to wrap my mind around the question *why? Why was this happening to me at that moment? Why would this guy who knew nothing about me go through all this trouble just to deny me the chance to tryout?*

I simply couldn't understand why he didn't just break the news the first time when I visited his office and asked about the program. If he already knew he had no intentions of giving me a chance for whatever reason, why didn't he just save us both the trouble and say no from the beginning? Yes, I probably would have questioned him and probably insisted on an opportunity to showcase my skills, but in the end, it was still his decision whether I made the roster or not. Either way, I would have respected his decision and moved on with my life.

After hearing what he had to say, I simply walked out of his office without a word. I was extremely disappointed and somewhat upset, but honestly, I wasn't surprised or shocked by what happened. Looking back at that moment, my disappointment wasn't so much about not making the team or the fact I was stripped of my opportunity to tryout. Yes, it would've been great to match up against Division I players and test myself. Yes, it would have been even greater to make the team if I had proven to be a good enough soccer player. Yes, a partial or a full athletic scholarship would have made a world of a difference in my life. Unfortunately, that did not happen.

I was disappointed mostly about the fact this coach intentionally went through so much trouble just to mislead me and get my hopes up for nothing. He strung me along for weeks and waited until right before the season started to say "No you're not good enough." He did all of that and made a decision without even seeing me play once. *Why? Because they get players from Europe?*

Those words stuck with me for a while. Imagine the disappointment after learning someone may have made up their mind about you and come to a conclusion about something important to your life in advance, but still chose to instead get your hopes up and string you along. Imagine looking forward to an opportunity to simply showcase your talents and then be denied without merit. Imagine simply asking for an opportunity to participate in something you deeply care about and being denied without a reasonable explanation. Instead, you're insulted because you're not who they want you to be. That's exactly how I felt about that entire situation.

Despite the terrible experience I had with the soccer program, my decision to attend Canisius was the right one. There is no doubt in my mind attending Canisius was the best academic decision I could have possibly made for my future. The school simply had one of the best academic curricula in the region and a talented pool of teachers. I'm not saying everything was smooth sailing throughout my two years at the school but overall I was in the right place at the right time and it was an amazing academic experience.

Initially, I had some difficulties adjusting to the much more challenging and demanding nature of a four-year school. As a transfer student from a community college, I had to navigate most of those challenges on my own as usual. Financially it was difficult to take on a $30,000 annual tuition most of which was covered by student loans. Had I opted to move onto campus into the dormitory for the full college experience instead of commuting, the price tag would have easily reached over $40,000 a year.

I qualified for some financial assistance and government educational grants, but they were not enough to cover the majority of my tuition. Accessing and retrieving the proper information for those programs and completing the application process was exhausting and sometimes a nightmare. But without loans and grants there was no way I would have been able to afford attending Canisius. During this process I discovered my eligibility for the Educational Opportunity Program was still viable. Apparently, I missed the window of opportunity to apply for the program during my first year at ECC and because of that I was still under the impression I could never apply for EOP again. I thought the missed opportunity was long gone until I transferred to Canisius.

It's true had I applied and been accepted into the program at the ECC, my benefits would have automatically transferred to Canisius and helped pay a reasonable portion for my tuition. However, because this wasn't the case, I had to provide documentation proving I qualified for the program during my first year of eligibility. If so, I would be permitted to apply for the program at Canisius as a new transfer student.

That was great news and a pleasant surprise. I was happy about a second opportunity to apply for the program and hoped to receive the much-needed help paying for tuition. First thing I did was ask about all the requirements to complete the application in time. I wasted no time in gathering all the necessary documents from the financial aid and EOP offices at ECC. I also gathered my parents' tax information, filled out the application as expeditiously as possible, and had it signed and delivered in time for processing.

The day I delivered that application to the counselor's office, I felt optimistic about my chances. I was a little nervous but I couldn't help but think about how much of a difference getting into the program would make in my academic career. Not only would it help pay for this very expensive school, I would be granted more access to other benefits the program provided.

When I arrived at the office I waited for some time before being invited in for a brief meeting with the counselor. I handed over my application and sat down at her desk across from her. She started to go through the application, and after reviewing a few pages of the document, she glanced at my application once more before turning to speak with me. She said, "There is a very long waiting list with over a hundred and fifty names. I don't know if you want to add your name to it." She continued and said, "I honestly didn't think it's worth putting your name on it because by the time you're close to the top of the it you will have already graduated."

I'm not quite sure what went through my mind when she said that, but I didn't question her assessment. I guess her suggestion made some sense. After all, I was a transfer student with only two years to go before graduating from Canisius. I thought, *Okay maybe she's right. What's the point of adding my name to the list if I'm not going to benefit from waiting all that time.* She handed my application back; I got up and walked away.

When I think back to that moment, I ask myself, *Why not add my application to the list anyway?" Why not become the one hundred fifty-first applicant? What was the worst THAT could have come from that simply action for me?* I don't have an answer to that question because there were no downsides to adding my name to the list. But there were plenty of benefits. I honestly don't know if the list was really that long to begin with but I trusted the counselor to guide me through this new and important process. I thought this person, whose job was to help advise and guide me through it, would do just that. I honestly thought she was doing her job by helping me make a decision that was in my best interest at that moment.

However, the questions for me remained: *Was she doing her job and was her advice in my best interest? Or was she doing what was in her best interest?* I thought she was looking to save me all the trouble of waiting for the much-needed financial assistance to help pay for my education. On the other hand, maybe she simply wanted to keep from adding anymore applications to her workload for that day. Maybe I happened to be unlucky number one hundred fifty-one, an unsuspecting kid who was doing his best trying to figure everything on his own. It's true I was open to accepting any help I could get at the time from just about anyone who was offering, and I thought the counselor was doing just that—helping. Regardless of her intentions that experience and the soccer team incident cast a dark cloud over my otherwise great academic career at Canisius.

I'm not looking to paint a picture of a naïve, unsuspecting, and gullible version of my young self through recounting these experiences. It is simply to share consequential moments in my life, particularly with respect to my education and how those moments impacted me. These two memories I shared about Canisius are experiences that warped the way I looked at the world and deal with people. I started to question people's intentions and motives more often than I used to after going through those experiences which was kind of difficult for me because I'm naturally more trusting than I am skeptical or suspicious of others. To grow and learn how to better protect myself from the world I had to accept life will sometimes challenge me in ways I may not know how to handle, but that does not mean I should take for granted or accept at face value the solutions others presented.

This was a particularly challenging period of my life but out of those challenges came many important life lessons and much personal growth. I will admit there were moments I felt I didn't belong at Canisius for other reasons besides the two detailed above. I focused on those two because they were the most consequential experiences. If things had played out differently in possibly one or both of those instances, I'm sure I would have been in a much better financial position for school. Thank God for my mother; she stepped up, like always, to help cover the cost of my education. If she didn't agree to take out additional loans for tuition, I would've had to leave Canisius. My point is there were times I wanted to give up or give in to all the challenges but I did not. I could not. Too many people had made sacrifices on my behalf particularly my mother, and I could not give up on her, on them or myself.

GRATEFUL FOR MY EDUCATORS

There were many more reasons to "stay in school" and keeping attending Canisius. These were the reasons I loved attending and often kept the idea of calling it quits at bay. First, I loved the academic programs and structure the school offered. As a political science major with a minor in international relations, I was exposed to a whole new academic world. I came in thinking I'm well-versed and I know enough about the world given my foreign and international background but I was wrong. In actuality I had very little exposure and knowledge to world affairs until I attended Canisius. All the introductory level courses drew me in and reignited my love for education. My level of interest grew in ways I hadn't experienced since I was a kid in Sudan. I was so excited to learn about political history, philosophy, international relations and American politics among many of other topics. I actually used to look forward to attending class regularly.

It's exciting to reflect on those days because it helps me truly appreciate what amazing educators we had at Canisius. I can't speak for every Canisius alumni but without a doubt in my mind, I had the pleasure of attending courses taught by some of the best professors in school. Most of my professors were extremely skilled at teaching their respective subject matter and had teaching methods that resonated with me.

My international relations (IR) professor was able to draw students into thought-provoking discussions in a special way. During his class, I was introduced to so many new concepts in ways that were simple to comprehend. He was also very approachable and made it easy to ask questions and have discussions during class or office hours.

Another one of my professors provided a unique international perspective and was insightful during her classes. Her teaching approach often felt more relatable to me personally and that may have something to do with our shared international backgrounds and experiences. She was also encouraging to all her students during class and dedicated tremendous amounts of time to making sure we understood the subject matter.

One professor introduced me to *The Daily Show* with Jon Stewart and I'm not sure there is a need to say much more besides that. Before that course I can't say for sure I was familiar with much of late-night TV satire. This professor used a combination of his vast knowledge on American politics and humor to engage students. I remember being fascinated with his teaching style and taking real genuine interest in American politics that semester. Needless to say after his class I watched a lot more of *The Daily Show* and *The Colbert Report* on a regular basis.

Last but certainly not least, is a professor I spent much of my memorable moments at Canisius in class with. He was an expert on the European Union (EU) and European affairs. He was also well-versed on American politics and world affairs but I enjoyed his course on the EU most. Through EuroSim, "an international, intercollegiate simulation of the European Union (EU)" I had the opportunity to travel to Europe for the first time with this professor and twelve classmates.[18]

The program brings together nearly two hundred students from fifteen colleges and university from the US and across Europe. Every year, a four-day conference is hosted in either the US or Europe and students participate in multiple student-driven policy making forums. I had the opportunity to participate in two EuroSim conferences, the first at Widener University in Chester, Pennsylvania. The second, was hosted by the University of Lower Silesia in Wroclaw, Poland. Both occasions were very informative and I very much enjoyed being a part of the diverse student body.

EUROSIM

In 2012, we traveled to Wroclaw, Poland for my second Euro-Sim experience at Canisius. I wasn't sure if I would be able to attend that year but I wanted to take part in the program for a second time during my last year at the school. I just didn't know if I would be able to scrape together the travel cost associated with the trip to Europe. The school provided accommodation, meals, and a number of other essentials for the trip but students were responsible for their own flight cost.

---

18   "TACEUSS, Trans-Atlantic Consortium for European Union Studies & Simulations EuroSim," *Canisius, Accessed March 5, 2021.*

Our round trip from the US and domestic travel cost into Europe amounted to about $1,100–$1,300. It was a great deal even by today's standard, for an international trip across the Atlantic Ocean plus travel cost between four European cities. However, for a full-time student working a part-time job at a community center, it was still too high of a price.

I knew I couldn't come up with the money on my own before the due date and I couldn't ask my mother for help. First, she had her own fiscal responsibilities that drained whatever little amount money she managed to put aside, namely supporting family back home in Sudan and Egypt. Second, if I ever asked, I knew she would go above and beyond to try supporting me even though she was in no position to do so. Lastly, my stepfather and I had all but stopped speaking by that point and my pride would not allow me to ask him for anything. Still, I was determined to explore all options to make this work.

I turned to the one person I can always count on for advice direction, prayer and support—Father Ron. I went to *Abuna*—Father Ron—and explained to him the predicament I was in. I told him I was excited about my opportunity to travel to Europe for the first time in my life, and about the added value EuroSim contributes to my degree program and education. Once I'd concluded my pitch, *Abuna* beginning asking about the program to better understand EuroSim and how might he be able to help.

In the classic *Abuna* fashion, once he understood my problem was all about funding, he started brainstorming about ways to help. As our conversation went on, *Abuna* paused for a second and then said to me, "Okay Jay, let me see what ROTA can do to help." I wasn't entirely sure what he meant exactly but I took comfort in his words as I often did. I knew even if there was nothing he could do to help, *Abuna* would give it his best and exhaust all options trying and that meant a lot to me.

Some people are fortunate enough to have people in their lives they can look to for support and direction individuals they confide in. Some have two or three they can always turn to, and others don't. I'm lucky enough to have a few trust-worthy individuals in my life who I can always rely on for just about anything. These people I consider to be guardian angels placed in my life for a higher purpose.

Abuna has been one of those people for most of my life in Buffalo. He has been a father figure, a mentor, and an excel-lent teacher. I've learned from him selflessness and dedication to serving God through the work we do in service to others is powerful. I've learned from *Abuna* compassion is not a weakness. It is a unique gift and a blessing from God that should be embraced and recognized for what it is: the best part of humanity. I've learned from *Abuna* so much more from simply watching him work with people throughout the community over the years. I've watched him treat each and every one he meets with the same level of respect and love regardless of who they were. His work ethic and willingness to constantly give and go above and beyond for someone in need is admirable.

We often used to joke about me one day becoming a Catholic priest and joining the brotherhood of the young men he has helped into priesthood over the years. I would always respond, "*Inshallah, Abuna*," meaning "God willing" in Arabic. Every time I said it, I truly meant it. I didn't know what God had in store for me at the time and I am still not one hundred percent sure how God wants me to dedicate my life. I may not follow *Abuna's* footsteps into priesthood like Reverend Father Daniel, Moses, and Denning—all now ordained Catholic priests. But I believe whatever God has in store for me will eventually come to pass.

My destiny may be through community organizations such as Reaching Out 2 Africa (ROTA), the non-profit founded by Father Ron in the 1990s for refugee assistance. It may be through other organization such as Shufto Soccer Initiative, Inc. a youth sports organization I founded in 2019 to work with kids and young adults on the soccer pitch. [19] Whatever it happens to be, I will welcome it with open arms in hopes of making a difference in the lives of others, just like *Abuna* and my other educators have made in my life.

---

19   "Shufto Soccer Initiative, Inc.," Shufto Soccer, Accessed March 5, 2021.

CHAPTER 18

Traveling 2012

———

The year 2012 was by far the most exciting during my college days. I had the opportunity to travel to Europe not once, but twice. I walked across the stage in front of my family and friends to receive my bachelor's degree (BA) in political science and international relations. I was the first of my siblings to do so which was important for the eldest child in the family. I then took to the sky later that year and traveled to the United Kingdom, Egypt, and to South Sudan for the first time since I was a toddler. Through EuroSim earlier that year I had visited Poland and Germany which brought the total number of countries I'd visited during that year to five. It was an exciting year.

My first international trip that year was for EuroSim to Poland. My group traveled through Canada on a flight from the German airline Lufthansa. We arrived in Düsseldorf, Germany first from Toronto Pearson International Airport in the early morning hours of the next day and awaited our connecting flight to Wroclaw, Poland. We then made our way to different parts of the airport in preparation for our next flight to Poland. It was snowing that early morning just like in Buffalo and Toronto, but for some reason it felt completely different from the western New York snow I'd grown used to all these years.

My classmates and I, along with our chaperone professor were all in the same area waiting for our flight. We were all gathered on one side of the room and on the other side standing possibly fifteen feet away or so from us was a man. He was standing alone with an airport cart filled with luggage. He looked African but I couldn't tell exactly where he may have been from. If I were to guess I'd say he looked West African. His complexion, facial features and build resembled some of my West African friends and so I assumed he was mostly likely from Liberia.

Along came a German airport security guard and he approached the man and asked him for his passport. The man gave his passport to the security guard, and the guard flipped through the pages of the book, presumably to check for proper visa stamps or citizenship. After a few moments, the guard handed the man his passport and walked away. I watched from where I was standing simply out of curiosity.

As he walked away, the security guard started walking directly toward me. At that moment my attention was split between my group and the interaction between the guard and the man across the room. However, when he started approaching my direction, I immediately shifted all my attention toward him. Once he approached me, the guard started speaking German. I don't speak German but I didn't need to know the language to understand what he was saying. From his hand gestures and from watching his interaction with the man across the room moments before, I figured he was asking for my passport as well. I replied in English and asked "Do you want to see my passport?" while I waved it in the air. He nodded and stuck his hand out.

I handed my passport to the security guard and after flipping through a few pages, he returned it back to me. At that moment I didn't see anything wrong with what had just transpired I thought he was doing a routine part of his job. I thought he was starting with me because I was the closest person to him from the group and he would make his way to check everyone else's passport before carrying on with his business. That's not what happened. After he checked my passport, he walked out of the room without even making eye contact with anyone else. I was puzzled. I turned to my group and asked "Did anyone just see that?" A few of them inquired and asked "See what?"

I explained the guard had just asked me for my passport, checked it, and walked away. One of my classmates asked "Really?" I answered "Yes." I explained before he walked over to me, he went to the gentleman across the room and asked him for his passport first. At this point, most of my group was paying attention to my account of what just occurred and seemed shocked. But I wasn't. I was just trying to keep from thinking about being racially profiled an hour or so after arriving in Europe for the first time. I didn't want to get upset about it but in the back of my mind I thought about how the gentleman across the room and I were the only Black African men in the room and we were the only ones asked to hand over our passports.

EUROSIM 2012

When we arrived in Wroclaw, I was no longer thinking about the airport incident at Düsseldorf. Instead, I was now looking forward to the four-day conference ahead and to the opportunity to meet students from across Europe. I was focused on the learning and the overall experience awaiting us in Poland.

Wroclaw was a beautiful city with a unique European feel to it with amazing aged structures all around town. I loved seeing the beautiful gothic cathedrals and parish churches I have not seen anywhere outside of Europe. I enjoyed learning about the city's history, the Polish people, the food and the beer.

I was genuinely enjoying my experience in Poland, but at the same time I couldn't help but feel the need to remain somewhat guarded at all times. Having lived in the United States since age of eleven the idea of being "the other" was a lingering feeling that was difficult to forget. I always felt I needed to have my guard up to protect myself from people who viewed me as "the other."

What this means is people who do not know or may be unfamiliar with your experience can often view and treat you as an outsider or an "other." Most immigrants and refugees have been subjected to harsh treatment and abused for being who they are and that's a difficult thing to forget. The feeling of being told directly or indirectly you are an "other," an outsider and don't belong is traumatic. People often experience this through overt racism and prejudiced acts directed against them, and other times through ignorant behavior by people who may not necessarily know the harm caused by their words or actions.

I've experienced both methods of being told "you are an other and you don't belong." I'd experienced it as a child in Sudan growing up. I'd experienced it in Egypt when we lived there, and I've experienced it in the US over the years. Prior to my American experience I didn't have an in-depth understanding of what racism was or why people held racist views toward each other. My lack of understanding was due partly to my young age and the other was a result of a combination of things. Having been born in one country, living in another for a period of time, and then growing up in a completely different part of the world makes my experience with racism multifaceted and more complicated than the experiences of most people.

Dealing with the reality of racism is an ongoing struggle for people like myself. Similar to victims of all kinds of traumatic events, such as war and violence and abuse, it is sometimes extremely difficult to move past these experiences. You have to learn to cope with the trauma and find ways to live and deal with it, knowing it always will be in the back of your mind.

So far, the only place I've felt the lowest levels of anxiety and safe enough to let down my guard was in South Sudan specifically in Malakal. It's a sad but true reality. The reason I felt safe there and not the "other" is because I felt at home in Malakal more than I have anywhere else in the world. Although I was not born or raised there, my mother and father were. My grandparents and my family members have a long and deep connection to the land as well as my *Cøllø* community. It is a part of our ancestral homeland and I felt that connection through the people living there. I felt at home because the people there did not look at me differently, nor did they treat me any different then they treated one another.

During my visit to Malakal, my cousins invited me to go with them to a *Nadi* one day, which is a sort of lounge or hangout spot they often went to. There they played games such as dominos and card games and there was always hot tea available. It was a good place to relax, ease your mind and forget about your troubles while staying sober. The day my cousins and I went, I was still new to town and had not yet met some of their friends.

One of the guys noticed my unfamiliar face and seemed curious to learn who I was and where I was coming from but didn't seem sure about how to ask. I did not participate in any of the games and decided to sit beside them as observer. I kept to myself, trying to read the room and did not say anything throughout. I wanted to simply be a fly on the wall and take it all in.

Most of the guys in the room paid no mind to me and carried on about their business. They were enjoying each other's company and using colorful language in *Dhok Cøllø (Shilluk)*. I was fascinated by all that was happening around me because until that point, it had been years since I was in an environment where people around me spoke my native tongue. Not since 1999 the year we immigrated to Egypt had I heard people speak my language so casually. So, I continued to sit and listen trying my best not to draw any attention.

My *Cøllø* language skills were still very rusty to say the least, but I was still able to understand and speak relatively well. Considering it had been over a decade since I last held a real conversation with anyone in *Dhok Cøllø*, my mother included, I was a lost cause. I definitely couldn't keep up with the guys because they were obviously much more proficient and comfortable speaking our language, but I was willing to try my best. It was going to be a struggle to keep up and I would have to ask in Arabic on occasion for some words to be translated but that wasn't going to deter me. I wanted to make sure I left Malakal with a much better command of my native tongue than when I first arrived.

As I sat nearby watching the guys play cards and dominos, the young man curious to figure out who I was, kept gazing in my direction. He had an increasingly puzzled look on his face and wanted to say something, but still was not sure what to ask. He waited for a bit before turning to one of my cousins and finally asking "*O-dong men kall-a-keny*?" which roughly translates to "Where did this Equatorian come from?" At that exact moment, all my cousins broke out in uncontrollable laughter. Without realizing it I also started laughing about his question. The only person who wasn't laughing was the young man himself. He had an increasingly puzzled look on his face and wondered why my cousins and I were all laughing about his question in *Dhok Cøllø*.

It took a moment for it to register in his mind that either I was aslo *Cøllø* and didn't look it, or I must have been an Equatorian, someone from the southern regions of South Sudan who spoke *Dhok Cøllø*. Either way, it was hilarious not because he didn't think I was *Cøllø*, but because I'd grown used to everyone thinking I'm from every other tribe except my own. It was an innocent moment I experienced without the dark and uncomfortable lingering feeling that usually accompanies being labeled an "other." I knew the kid had no bad intentions in asking his question nor was he trying to be tribalist. He was curious about me because of my unfamiliar face and genuinely didn't know the best way to ask his question.

I've had people ask if I was Senegalese because of my dark complexion, and I've had people ask if I was born in the US because I spoke "good English." Each time someone asks a question pertaining to my background and ancestral roots I'm glad to share those details with them. I believe most people are genuine and want to simply learn about me and my background.

However, some people are not. I find it sometimes difficult to take the same approach with people who make unfaltering assumptions about whom they believe I am, without making any attempts to first ask. I often try not to respond negatively to someone saying, "You speak good English for an African," or "Wow, you don't have an accent for an African," or even "You are very well-spoken for an African."

Hearing those comments makes me wonder whether people think about the meaning behind words before uttering them. I've had people ask me questions about my place of birth and then be surprised to discover someone like me can adopt an American accent without having been born in this country. Then they are shocked to learn English is not my first nor second, but actually my third language. Most shocking is the idea my intelligence can somehow be measured through my accent.

The idea someone is smarter than the next simply because of how they pronounce a word or utter a sentence is ridiculous. I've seen people try to belittle someone because they had a thick accent and uplift another because they did not. Those experiences along with countless others have forced me to develop a sort of defense mechanism which keeps me on high alert and always mindful of my surroundings.

That's a reality many refugees and immigrants have to deal with regularly. It's an experience you constantly have to relive in many places outside of wherever you feel truly at home. When I traveled to Germany and Poland, I was reminded of that reality just hours after landing in Europe. For the duration of my trip there, I felt the need to keep myself on guard.

A CONVERSATION WITH MY FATHER

On Tuesday February 7, 2012 I called my father to check on him and to make sure he was doing well. We'd started trying to rekindle our relationship just months before after years of not having spoken a word to one another. Following that conversation I decided to write down my thoughts and feelings about what was said. Here they are:

I just got off the phone with my father whom I have not spoken with in a few months. He is in Malakal, Upper Nile State in South Sudan, and he told me he has just arrived back from the capital, Juba. Currently he is mobile between the two cities, Malakal and Juba, and on occasion travels to Khartoum where he owns another home. Dad is still unemployed as a result of his involvement in politics, particularly last year's contentious election. Despite being a half a world away from him and not having seen him in about thirteen or fourteen years, I feel comfortable talking with him about all that's happening in his life and mine.

Honestly, I'm not sure what he looks like now and I don't even remember exactly what he looked like when we left Sudan for Egypt. I still feel comfortable talking with him though and I guess that's probably because he is my father after all. Also, being the type of person I am probably makes it easier to talk to because I can't and don't hold grudges against people, not even him.

A lot of people in my position would be quite angry with their fathers if they had a relationship similar to ours. That's only if you can even call it a relationship. I don't have much to say about my father, nothing bad at least. I don't remember much about him either. I was young when he visited me occasionally back in Khartoum and during those visits, I don't think we once had a memorable father-son moment. I remember my aunty, his second-youngest sister whom, along with her family, were the closest family members I had from his side. She is the best and I can't wait to visit her once I go back home.

Back to the reason I am writing tonight at this late hour on a school night. Shortly before calling my father for the first time this year, I was thinking about ways to improve my grades this semester. It was the final semester of my undergraduate years at Canisius College. I was also thinking about my next move after graduation. I had somewhat started making up my mind about taking a full year off and returning for a master's degree in international relations, or something in that arena.

My plans for the summer were to try securing an internship at a law firm a parishioner at the St. Martin de Porres used to work at as a paralegal. He recommended me to the firm and I intended on taking the opportunity to get a firsthand learning experience at a firm. Unfortunately, I was unable to secure the internship during my last semester as I hoped but I was able to secure a part-time job instead.

I was planning on taking the opportunity to learn whether studying law was really my passion, or whether I was destined to study something different. At the same time I was quite mindful of the fact I had to prepare myself for my long-awaited trip back to Africa. To prepare, I needed to earn some money to pay for my round trip. My part-time job at the Belle Center served as an opportunity for a full-time position during the summer and a chance to work with the kids maybe for the last time. The Belle Center by the way was a great place for any child, teen, or adult to go for a verity of programs. I enjoyed my time there as an AmeriCorps Volunteer serving the community and as an employee working with school-age kids and other older groups except during the winter.

SUMMER 2012

During the summer of 2012 I was unemployed for the first time in a long time. Previously, I had worked as a youth employee for my church at the age of fourteen or fifteen, and I continued to work, mostly on a part-time basis during high school and into college. I sometimes worked two jobs during the summer when I had more time on my hands, so it was quite bizarre and somewhat aggravating to be unemployed right after graduation.

It was more frustrating to not be able to meet my financial obligations and struggling to take care of myself. I had always managed to take care of myself since I got my first job and I took great pride in it. Given the conditions and state of the of the US economy at the time it was difficult for many recent college graduates to find decent jobs especially in my field of political science and international relations.

It was difficult to find work with decent pay even in other fields like manual labor. Thankfully at the time I was living with my family so I didn't have to worry much about my living arrangements or paying rent. For two months I was basically spending most of my time at home watching political analysts commenting on who should be elected president of the United States. Democrats argued in favor of and defended President Obama's policies, while their counterparts criticized the president and tried making a case for Governor Romney and the (GOP) Republican Party. Even though I was a political science major, I didn't realize how polarizing American politics were becoming until that point.

During that same time I contemplated and considered exploring all my options to find a job including the possibility of relocating. Top on my list was moving to the nation's capital, Washington DC. I had hoped to land a decent entry-level position in my field of study, which would have been the best-case scenario. I was also open to the possibility of accepting an internship, granted it was a paid internship, so I may be able to provide for myself.

I tried to secure one or the other and tapped into the Canisius alumni network in the capital all the way toward the end of the summer of that year. I was convinced DC would be the best location to move to compared to other major cities with potential employment opportunities in my field of study such as New York City or somewhere abroad. I was sold on DC since my first visit through school with a group of my undergraduate political science and international relations majors the previous year.

We had an opportunity to meet with high-level government officials and top executives in the private sector. We also met with mid-level officials and recent graduates in the midst of starting their careers in the capital. They were all Canisius alumni who ended up in Washington, DC and they shared insight from their personal experiences and advised, encouraged, and welcomed each and every one of us to reach out if we needed any help.

Unfortunately, things did not work out according to plan and finding and securing a paid internship or an entry-level position proved more difficult than I imagined. I reached out to our alumni network on multiple occasions asking for assistance and some people were very helpful with giving direction and leads, but no opportunity materialized. I was advised by some alumni to pack up and move down to DC because that would improve my chances of landing an internship and could have potentially led to a job at a later time. I seriously considered doing just that, but the idea of moving somewhere like DC without accommodation or anyway to provide for myself was unthinkable.

Needless to say, life after graduation didn't allow me to relocate to Washington, DC or anywhere else for that matter—not without a job. Instead, I decided to venture halfway across the world to visit my family most of whom I have never met before in my life. I decided to travel back home to South Sudan, formally the southern region of war-torn Sudan. By that time in 2012, South Sudan was an independent country no longer a part of a united Sudan.

One year before I visited, the country successfully split in 2011 after decades of bloodshed and civil war. The South now held the title of being the world's newest nation, a title proudly welcomed by most South Sudanese at home and in the diaspora around the world. Very few people including myself imagined South Sudan ever gaining independence, let alone during our lifetime.

South Sudan's independence was comparable to the election of President Barrack Obama to the United States presidency in 2008. South Sudanese around the world felt similar to how most Americans particularly African Americans felt during Obama's election. That feeling of witnessing history in the making and seeing America elect not only its first black President, but someone who reflected the changing times of this country was powerful. Most South Sudanese felt similarly about independence from a repressive regime and a system that imposed a second-citizen structure, war, and policies that denied their collective will for decades. July 9, 2011 was a new beginning for the South and a sign for a hopeful and bright future South Sudanese to look to for years to come, a sentiment I shared as a son of the South.

LONDON TO MALAKAL

I packed my bags for a two-month journey from the US through the UK to South Sudan. Filled with excitement, I decided it would be best to make the most of this journey and visit family in a few countries along the way. The first location on my list was London to visit family living in the United Kingdom. From the UK I would travel to Egypt to visit more family living there whom I had not seen since leaving Sudan. From Egypt to the capital of South Sudan, Juba. I had never been to Juba before and I was looking forward to my time there before leaving the capital for Malakal which was my final destination.

The journey from Buffalo, New York to Malakal, and from Malakal back to Buffalo spanned roughly eight weeks in total. I first arrived at London Heathrow Airport filled with excitement and looking forward to my time in the English capital. After a six-hour flight via British Airways, I arrived safely in England the next morning. I was surprisingly alert and filled with energy despite the fact I did not sleep on the plane. It was exciting to have finally made it to London after months of anticipation and I looked forward to exploring the city. At the customs and security check point, I arrived with my laptop bag and a small carry on. I said good morning to the agent and she asked for my passport which I had it readily available and handed over. The officer then proceeded to ask seemingly routine questions which I then answered.

Officer: "Where are you traveling from?"

Me: "I'm coming from Buffalo, New York."

Officer: "What's the purpose of your visit to the UK?"

Me: "I'm here visiting my family."

Officer: "How long will you be staying in the UK?"

Me: "Just about a week, then I'm going to Africa."

Officer: "How long exactly will you be here and what's the address you will be staying at?"

Me: "I'll be staying here for about six or seven days, and I don't actually know my cousin's address. They will be picking me up from the airport so I didn't ask."

Officer: "You're traveling to a foreign country, and you don't know the address you will be staying at?"

Officer: "What is your occupation?"

Me: "I recently graduated from college and don't have a job yet."

Officer: "How can you afford to travel without a job?"

Me: "I worked prior to this trip."

By that point it had been a few minutes and I was beginning to get a bit frustrated with her line of questioning and her increasingly demeaning tone. I was trying my best to be as honest and straight forward as possible, and I understood she was trying to do her job. I'd watched her deal with a few different passengers before me and her interaction was completely different.

The agent continued to ask more questions that were increasingly personal and seemingly irrelevant, and I couldn't help but start to react a bit defensively. I didn't say anything out of line but my facial expressions probably said a lot. Eventually I was cleared and free to go. As I walked toward the airport's exit, I wondered what that was all about and why the officer felt the need to basically interrogate me about my visit. I thought surely, she is familiar with and probably deals with US citizens visiting the UK fairly often. Besides, I had explained and shown proof I'm only visiting for a short period before leaving for Africa the following week. The situation reminded me of my experience at Düsseldorf International Airport earlier that year when the

German airport officer approached me and the only other Black man in the room to check our travel documents. Once again, I had to try my best not to let that derail my overall experience in the UK.

My cousins were gracious enough to show me around London and make the best of my time with them. However, one major issue I struggled with was driving on the left side of the road. I personally did not get behind the wheel, but I did suffer from a case of heightened anxiety whenever I was in the passenger side of the vehicle. The first few days in London were brutal whenever we drove anywhere especially when on the road for an extend period of time. Overall, I enjoyed sightseeing and the view over London from up high aboard the London Eye and visiting places such as the Natural History Museum.

My visit to the UK quickly came to an end as expected and off to the airport I went. My flight through Egypt was a transit stop between London and Juba. I had a layover in Cairo until my next flight, and this was my first time back on Egyptian soil since we left the country over a decade ago. I planned on paying a brief visit to my aunt and uncles and their children whiles in Cairo, but that was not possible until I returned from South Sudan, which I did about five or six weeks later.

On my way back from Juba, I notified my aunt I had a seventeen- to eighteen-hour layover in Cairo. I told her I would be staying in a hotel near the airport until it was time to board my next flight back to London. On the flight from Juba I was seated next to a South Sudanese young man also making his way back to London following a visit with his family in Juba. He and I struck a conversation regarding history, politics, tribalism, business, and a range of topics concerning South Sudan. He seemed full of life and excitement about the future of the country just like I was and our ongoing conversation made the flight to Cairo much more interesting.

We landed in Cairo around 10:00 or 11:00 p.m. later that night and boarded an airport shuttle to the nearby hotel. Before landing, I shared with my new travel companion my plans to visit my family in the morning and return to the airport for the flight to Heathrow. I also floated the idea of visiting the pyramids and asked if he had any plans that morning or if he wanted to join me instead. He didn't have anything planned and intended on waiting for the flight to London at the hotel. I told him "Okay, you're more than welcome to join me tomorrow morning."

The following morning I woke up bright and early in time for breakfast and a road trip to visit my family and the Great Pyramid of Giza. My new friend and I met at the breakfast table enjoyed our meals, and hired a taxi driver. After negotiating a flat price, the driver agreed to drive us to both destinations and back to the airport in time for our next flight. He was adamant about getting paid in US dollars.

I didn't know the exchange rate at the time and I didn't bother looking it up. Frankly I was more concern with my visit to see family and to the Pyramids in time before our flight. So I agreed to pay him $50 for the round trip and to add gratuity once we were back at the airport. The driver was extremely happy about that arrangement because he ended up earning about 360 Egyptian pounds in a matter of hours.

In Cairo, finding your way around town can be extremely difficult and frustrating for anyone not familiar with the city. If you don't speak Egyptian Arabic it can be nerve-racking. Fortunately, I retained a decent amount of my Egyptian

Arabic over the years, enough to communicate with the taxi driver but I also had my aunt speak with him over the phone for directions.

Unlike most cities in the Western Hemisphere, directions in Cairo are based on street intersections, landmarks, markets, and other structure familiar to locals. They are not often based on street addresses. Most taxi drivers in Cairo knew exactly where to go based on directions provided, and we were able to make it to my aunt's home in no time.

It was exciting to see my aunt Sara whom I hadn't since Khartoum. She is my mother's youngest sister and it had been over twelve years since we had seen each other. She was now a mother and I was pleased to meet my little cousin for the first time. I had a few presents and gifts my mother asked me to deliver that I had been carrying around, and I was happy to finally give them to her.

She offered my new friend the taxi driver, and myself hot tea and water, which is customary, and asked us to also stay for lunch. I explained as much as I would love to stay and continue to catch up since it's been ages, I can't unfortunately because of our tight schedule.

It was difficult having to leave so soon after just having arrived at her home and I truly wanted more time to spend with her and her daughter after all these years. I wanted to reflect on old times because she and I used to get along very well growing up. It was interesting to see the shared similarities she now had, both in resemblance and character with my mom. They are both down to earth and easy to get along with, and they are also both straight forward and brutally honest sometimes. Most importantly, they both shared a loving nature toward family and friends. I missed that most about her.

As difficult as it was, I had to say my goodbyes to Aunt Sara and her young daughter before hitting the road toward Giza. I didn't have a game plan for the Pyramids nor did my new friend because he had never been to Egypt before then. Along the way our taxi driver started to pitch both of us a special tourist deal that he could secure for a special price only guaranteed through his associates working near the pyramids.

Having lived in Egypt in the past, I was familiar with how persistent Egyptians can be with their aggressive sales techniques. I knew immediately our driver was pulling the "jack of all trade" card on us which was typical. Fortunately for him I was more concerned with my time than with the price on a "great deal" and he was doing a good job so far keeping us on schedule so I agreed. I agreed to pay for the special package because I was aware if he could maximize his earning potential that day especially in US dollars, he would be willing to go above and beyond for my friend and me if needed.

We finally arrived in Giza at a distance I can see the Pyramids. I realized that was my very first time seeing them in my life and it was an amazing sight. Having lived in Cairo over a decade before, I remembered no one talked about sightseeing around Egypt or going to see the pyramids. It reminded me of Niagara Falls and some Buffalo natives. Although Buffalo, New York is about a twenty-five-minute drive from Niagara Falls, one of the largest waterfalls and wonders in the world, I know people who have never once visited. I know people who were born and raised in Buffalo and nearby towns across western New York who haven't made the short drive to the Falls. I was reminded of my own similar experience with the Great Pyramid of Giza in my back yard while living in Egypt.

Our taxi driver directed us to an area that seemed filled with more locals than tourists and introduced us to a gentleman in charge of a horse and camel ride business. There was a young man no older than twelve or thirteen years of age working with him, and he seemed familiar with the daily routine. The man asked my friend and I whether we wanted to ride a horse or a camel and we both chose horses. I've never gone horseback riding before, nor have I climbed onto the back of a camel. My new friend like me didn't seem to have any prior experience either. We both agreed the horses were a good start because riding a camel seemed like it required a bit more of a skill we certainly didn't have.

We got on the horses and the young man began directing both horses on a pathway toward the three Giza Pyramids. Both horses were doing just fine at first and walked down a path I assumed was familiar to them. The path was on an upward incline, and the boy guided both horses as we continued to walk toward the pyramids. At some point along the way the boy's attention shifted toward my friend's horse because it required more control. At that moment he decided to hand me my horses' reins and I was left to my own devices.

It was an unexpected move, and I had to quickly adjust to the situation. I actually didn't mind being in full control of my horse but what I was a bit concerned about was the fact my horse was walking very close to the edge. If you've seen a photo of the Great Sphinx of Giza, you have probably seen one of the great pyramids behind it. That is the pyramid of Khafre or Chefren, the second largest of the three pyramids.

What you may not have noticed in any of those photos is the inclined pathway leading to the pyramid of Khafre along the left side of the Sphinx. That pathway has an excellent view of the Sphinx from above but it does not have any guard railing to protect you from a steep fall off the edge. My horse was walking up about one foot (.3048) or maybe less from the edge, and all I could do was to keep directing the horse to left. I kept telling myself "Don't panic and don't make any sudden moves. Trust the horse will walk up the path safely for the next couple of minutes and the Sphinx will not be your last sight in this world."

Thankfully we both made it up the incline to the Pyramid of Khafre in one piece. It was truly a magnificent sight to see up close and put into perspective why they're considered one of the seven wonders of the world. For a few minutes I took in the magnitude of what I was seeing for the first time, and soon after we took some *touristy* pictures on the pyramids before making our way down. This time however, I didn't not have to worry about my horse walking on the edge and I was grateful for that.

Once we were back on the ground, our taxi driver was ready to take us back to the airport. We were cutting it close on time, and the drive to the airport was about an hour long. The flight out of Cairo to London was scheduled to depart in less than two hours, and my buddy and I needed to be there in time to clear security. Fortunately, we both had our carry-on bags and did not need to go back to the hotel and we made it to the airport just in the nick of time. When we got there, security did not want to let us through because we were running extremely late but after pleading with him for some time, he agreed to clear us for entrance and we rushed to catch our flight. We arrived at the gate just thirty minutes or so before departure and boarded the flight just in time to make it back to London.

CHAPTER 19

Juba to Malakal

———

I arrived at Juba International Airport on Thursday, December 6, 2012. It was a bright, sunny, hot afternoon and the weather felt still and humid. Juba, now the capital of an independent South Sudan was going through juristic change at that time. There were also many challenges that needed to be addressed as to be expected of any capital of a new nation. Most surprising was the fact some of those major issues were evident from the moment you landed at the airport.

The first sight I laid my eyes on while stepping out of the airplane was the large new airport terminal that seemed to still be under construction. It was a good sign there were important infrastructure projects underway but it was a little shocking the airport hadn't been completed already. The second thing I noticed was the actual airport terminal all of the arriving passengers were instructed to walk toward for customs and bagging claim. From outside the building, it appeared pretty small but normal beside the new terminal under construction. However, once I entered the building it quickly became apparent navigating through it would be a major issue.

This single building served as the only space for everything at the arrival terminal at Juba International Airport.

On one side of the building—the right side upon entering—I saw a huge crowd of people standing in an oval-shaped gathering waiting for their luggage. In the middle of the gathering were a few airport employees placing luggage bags in the middle of the floor for owners to claim.

There was no baggage carousel in sight. Instead there was a single square-shaped hole on the wall with men from the outside of the building passing luggage to their coworkers on the inside. I didn't know what to think at that moment because I'd never seen anything like it, but there was no time to stand around and wonder because I had to quickly get with the program and look for my bags. It was now my responsibility just like everyone else, to keep an eye out for my luggage so I didn't lose track or worse, watch someone else walk away with it.

On the other end on the left side of the building was customs. Once you claimed your bags it was time to check in with customs. There were two lines leading to two windows with custom officers validating visas and passports. One line was designated for South Sudanese citizens and the other for foreigners. I was traveling with my American passport but there was no clear indication as to which line was which. People were moving freely from one line to the other and cutting in line wherever they could.

I was a bit confused and wondered why no one waited their turn in line, and why no officer was there to enforce the rules to maintain order. I managed to keep my spot in line and eventually reached the front. The officer validating travel documents was behind a glass window with a small opening underneath it. I handed my passport over to him; he took my passport and before he opened the book, he looked intently at me and said in Arabic, "That's the line for foreigners," and pointed to the other line. I didn't respond because I had no idea what to say while waiting for his next move. He then checked my visa and after a few seconds he gave it back to me. He didn't say anything else. Instead, he indicated with his hand I was good to go by pointing toward the other end of the room. By the exit door full of people waiting to greet travelers was the security desk where they riffled through everyone's luggage.

Amongst the crowd of people standing by the exit door was my cousin *Jido*, now also known as Zero, and my aunt *Adut*. They were there waiting to welcome me to Juba. I'd never met Aunty *Adut* before that day and I was a little worried I may not recognize Zero because it had been nearly fourteen years since I'd last seen him. Luckily, Zero spotted me while I was still waiting for my luggage and I was able to recognize him.

He was now much taller than I remembered in Khartoum where we all lived before my family migrated to Cairo. Aunty *Adut* resembled Aunty Josephine and it was really nice to finally meet her. In Khartoum, I only knew Aunty *Nyibol*, Zero's mother and their family. We often visited with them and they were one of the two direct family members from my stepfather's side of the family I grew up around in Khartoum.

Now that I was in Juba, I had a chance to finally get a realistic and personal view of the capital of South Sudan, instead of having to rely heavily on news outlets depicting the state of the new country through their own lenses. I had a chance to see with my own eyes what the streets and new structure across Juba all looked like. I wanted a good idea of what people were doing and feeling during that pivotal moment in history.

I planned on staying in Juba for about a week-and-a-half before traveling to Malakal to spend Christmas and New

Year's Eve with my dad and grandfather. But I was filled with hope, excitement, and optimism about being in South Sudan. I had been closely following all the political developments in the country prior to and leading up to the referendum vote in January 2011. My interest in the country's affairs only increased after that point and it was amazing to celebrate Independence Day on July 9 of that same year. To finally set foot in the new country, a place all the South Sudanese people can claim and proudly call home was increasable. To be in Juba at that particular time was powerful.

MALAKAL

When I landed in Malakal, I didn't know what to expect. My only experience in South Sudan so far was with Juba's airports and I couldn't imagine things getting worst. Fortunately, Malakal isn't as populated as Juba and our flight was one of the few scheduled to arrive at the airport that day. When I exited the airplane the weather was noticeably cooler than it was in Juba. The sun was beaming, and I felt a pleasant breeze in the air that was much different from the humidity found in Juba. We made our way to the nearby building to wait for the luggage and that's when I noticed this terminal was also very different from the arrival terminal in the capital.

The terminal appeared bigger from outside, and once I entered the building my experience was quite different as well. Everything was less hectic and everyone at the Malakal airport came across as being much calmer. The difference felt almost similar to when we first arrived at Buffalo Niagara Airport after leaving JFK. The obvious differences of course being the level of development and infrastructure between the two countries.

The building's interior was also in good shape and looked like a reasonable small provincial airport. There were seating areas where passengers could wait for their luggage and the baggage carousel seemed to be in good shape but did not appear functional. As I waited for my luggage I couldn't help but think about the difference between the two airports, and I just hoped I didn't have to worry about receiving my bags in a similar fashion as I did in Juba.

Meanwhile, I decided to call my dad and tell him I had landed safely and was now at the airport waiting for my bags. When I called, he was in the middle of a workshop but said he would come pick me up in about thirty minutes. I told him it was fine; he did not have to leave the workshop to come get me I was willing to take a taxi to the house by myself I just needed the house address. He chuckled lightly and said "We don't have house numbers here."

For a moment, I felt a little silly for asking and didn't say anything else. I wasn't sure what to say and I started telling myself I had to make sure not to come across as some "westernized kid" that's going to need some sort of special treatment. I didn't want to be a pain to deal with around the rest of my family. I agreed to stay put at the airport and wait for him to come pick me up whenever he was free.

My suitcases finally arrived; I collected both of them and continued to wait for my ride. Twenty-five to thirty minutes later my dad showed up in this old Toyota Prado. It must have been an early '90s model and it looked like it had seen better days. In Juba, I'd seen countless newer models on the roads but none looked like my father's. He seemed content with his Prado and rightfully so, because very few people in South Sudan could afford a personal vehicle. I needed to be mindful not to compare, nor should I have been comparing my experience in South Sudan to my experience in the US.

Shortly after, my dad walked into the waiting hall where I was seated and greeted me with a firm handshake. He then helped load my luggage into the back of his Prado before we left the airport. I know it may seem that after not having seen me in over thirteen years a handshake would be inadequate or even inappropriate for such an occasion. Yes, in some cultures it would have been an intense and emotional reunion filled with hugs and kisses but not for us. The fact he and I never had a close father-son relationship to begin with did not help.

The house wasn't too far from the airport but the car ride made it seem further. The roads were quite bumpy and my dad was in a bit of a rush to get back to his medical workshop. He had to go back to the workshop after dropping me at the house and said he would be back in time for dinner in a few hours. I told him it was okay because I needed to relax a little bit once we were at the house anyway.

I called my grandfather earlier at the airport while I was waiting for my dad to show up. I told Grandpa I just arrived in Malakal and was waiting for dad to pick me up at the airport. My dad was aware my grandfather was in town near the market where they regularly see one another and would possibly come to the house to visit that same day. I figured we would most likely see each other sometime the following day.

That late afternoon I decided to take a nap outside under a shaded little structure attached to my dad's room. He had an *angareeb* there. An *angareeb* is a small, portable, wooden bed frame with a base made of woven rope that's popular in Sudan and South Sudan. I hadn't seen one in over a decade and I was happy to take a nap on it under the shade. Not long after I closed my eyes, I heard a loud banging on the metal front door. Immediately I jumped up on the *angareeb* and wondered who might be at the door. My father had keys for the door and no one else knew I was there yet. They banged on the door once more; that's when I reluctantly got up to answer the door.

It's difficult to put in words what I felt the moment I open the door, and it's even more difficult to express what my grandfather means to me. It had been so long since I last saw him, I wasn't prepared and had no clue how I might react when I did see him again. I also did not know how he might react when he saw me. The moment I opened the door and saw my grandfather, I immediately broke down.

Suddenly, I was overwhelmed with emotions and I couldn't help but break down. Grandpa was overwhelmed with emotions as well, and at that exact moment when we saw each other, it was clear how much we had both missed one another. This was the first time he has seen me since we left Sudan for Egypt in 1999. Here I was after all those years in flesh and blood standing before him no longer a small boy, but now a young man in my early twenties.

I hugged my grandfather with tears flowing down my cheeks, unable to remain calm and collected in the same manner I did when I first saw my father earlier that day. It was too incredible of a moment to act like it was business as usual upon seeing my one and only living grandparent.

I then invited Grandpa Samuel *Ayok* to come into the courtyard and have a seat. I offered him water and we started a conversation as if we hadn't been apart for over fourteen years. My grandfather and I always had a special, close relationship. All my life he has had a special place in my heart even though we were apart for so long. Growing up both my grandparents showed so much love but were also taught in their respective ways. Grandma was more of the disciplinarian compared to Grandpa, so naturally I got away with more things around him. He was a powerful figure in the household and a hard-working smart man. I like to think some of his traits trickled down to my siblings and me.

My mother used to tell me about her youth and about the comfortable life they had in Malakal in the '70s. Back then, some South Sudanese led simple but fairly decent life. Some parts of South Sudan were not yet ravished by civil war. In our region in Upper Nile State home to the *Cøllø* kingdom and its inhabitants, life was good. Mom would share her memories and talk about those days with a nostalgic tone and genuine happiness—the "good old days." She once told me Grandpa used to work with a guy named Fred, a white European man who worked for some organization that built schools throughout South Sudan.

In the past my mother used to tell me about the kind of parent he was growing up. She talked about how he would be gone sometimes for days or weeks on end for work. But whenever he returned home, he brought back gifts and treats from different regions of the country. She also talked about growing up in Malakal and regularly visiting her home village *"Kowg"* located directly across the White Nile from Malakal. Back then, everything they needed was available nearby and food was abundant. She would say, "There was plenty of fresh fish in the local market and everything else we needed was easily within reach."

Cøllø people are excellent fisherman and fish is one of the main staples in our diet. When Mom shared those memories, I often got excited about the experience because I had never been to the Malakal prior to my visit in 2012. I had no idea how excellent the quality of food was in the region and I very much looked forward to one day experiencing it. When I finally visited in 2012, I had the opportunity to put mom's words to the test. She did not exaggerate; it's been over thirty years since she was home and everything she described about the food tasting amazing was still true.

Grandpa and I continued our conversation, and the first hour went by without notice. Another thirty minutes or so went by as well. We were catching up and trying to understand each other's worlds in the limited time we had that day, but it was impossible to cover fourteen years of events in a matter of hours. As he spoke, he asked about Mom, my siblings, and *Jal Pownye*. It is the *Cøllø* word for teacher which he used to refer to my stepdad, Natale. I listen very intently as I used to always do as a kid when I listen to his stories. I answered his questions as best as I could and waited for his follow-up questions.

As we continued this back-and-forth dialogue, I couldn't help but notice how very little some things have changed despite the time that had passed. Grandpa looked slightly order and thinner than I remembered back in Khartoum, but he was still the towering figure I had always known him to be. His voice still sounded the same and his iconic laughter had not changed one bit.

I knew life in Sudan now South Sudan was still very difficult, but I didn't know for sure how that may have impacted my grandpa. He was now the only grandparent I had and I wanted to cherish every moment I had left with him. As I tried my hardest to remain in the present with Grandpa, I wondered when, if ever, I would be able to visit him again. I thought about visiting him along with my mother next time, and about what it would mean for her to see her father alive and well.

We continued talking for another hour or so and every time I appeared to start getting sentimental or a little bit emotional, Grandpa noticed and quickly said something funny. He then would start to laugh and I would start laughing also while trying to fight back tears. His big personality made it easy to be around him, and his infectious laughter brought back good memories from my childhood. He always had a way of lighting up a room and bringing out the best in everyone around him.

By now it's been nearly two-and-a-half hours since Grandpa showed up at the door, and he had to head back to town before sunset. I knew his time to leave was fast approaching, but I honestly didn't want him to go. It had been so long since he and I had a chance to see one another and I wanted to make the absolute most of our every moment together.

He started to explain in *Dhok Cøllø* our native language he had to make it back to town right away to cross the river and go back to the village before nightfall. Grandpa was now the chief in the village and had to attend to his responsibilities. I understood and reluctantly responded, "Okay." He was still pretty upbeat as he walked toward the front door and reminded me I must visit him in the village during the days ahead. He wanted me to see his home and meet the elders and my extended family. I agreed and said I was looking forward to it before he opened the door and started walking away.

My father came home about an hour after grandpa left, then we went out for dinner. It was a nice, cool evening at a local restaurant near the house. We didn't talk much about anything specific besides my plans while in Malakal for the next few weeks. I enjoyed being outdoors in the cooler evening temperatures of Malakal compared to the humid nights back in Juba.

The next morning my dad was leaving for anther full day at a workshop at Malakal Teaching Hospital. The medical facility is located near the town center on the eastern bank of the River Nile. I went with him that day and spent most of the afternoon writing and reflecting on my time in South Sudan so far. The following day I decided to visit my uncle and his family.

Uncle Daniel *Dak, Ogua* is a short man in stature shorter than I am which is pretty unusual in the land of "giants." However, he has a big personality and probably one of the best people I've met in Malakal and in my extended family. I had heard so much about him from my mother over the years but I had never met him in person. I was a little nervous but nonetheless looking forward to our first in-person meeting.

Mom is very fond of Uncle *Ogua* and she used to tell me about their childhood growing up in Malakal. He was a big brother and behaved like it as well. Mom shared stories about his no-nonsense approach to everything and how he was never to be taken lightly. As strict and bossy as he was toward his younger cousins and siblings in the household, he was kindhearted and fair. You could be angry with him for a moment but you could never hate nor hold a grudge against him. He was just that kind of guy and they all knew as the oldest brother he was doing what was in their best interest to protect them.

Mom often pointed out I am a lot like my uncle *Ogua*. Besides our height similarity she pointed out he and I share many characteristics. She hoped one day I would have a chance to meet him in person and see for myself. So now that I was in Malakal, the day had come to meet the man himself. When I finally met him, I was in awe of Mom's descriptions of my uncle because they were spot on.

Uncle *Ogua's* father was my grandpa Samuel's older brother who passed on before I was born. Grandpa raised Uncle *Ogua* and his siblings in the same household with my mother and her siblings. This is common practice in many Sudanese communities and so my mother and her cousins were very close growing up and remain so today. I was named after Uncle *Ogua's* father Grandpa *Olwak* and I wasn't not the only one. Mom used to also share childhood memories about Grandpa *Olwak* and she described him as an amazing figure beloved by everyone throughout the community.

Uncle *Ogua's* youngest son is also named *Olwak*. He was about two or three years old when I visited and he and I got along pretty well. We had a strong bond probably because we shared Grandpa *Olwak's* name and his great spirit. I called him Olwak *thean* (small), and he called me Olwak *dwong* (big). I really enjoyed the time I spent with all of them in Malakal. Not only was I surrounded by loving family members and felt truly at home, but I also was able to reflect on my life and reexamine what truly mattered and what did not.

One major event that occurred during my visit to Malakal was a family gathering organized on my behalf. My father and his extended family living in Malakal were all present at this dinner prayer. My beloved and late Aunty *Nyatow* was there as well along with Aunty *Nyamojwok*, and Aunty *Nyakwaj*. I was very happy to see Aunty *Nyatow* because I hadn't seen her, my two cousin's Bill and *Fajuan* or the rest of the family since Khartoum. I hadn't seen Aunty *Nyamojwok* since I was a little boy either. Aunty *Nyakwaj* I met for the first time during that visit to Malakal and it was a blessing meeting her and my cousins, her children. There were many other family members I was meeting for the first time including my older cousins and their families. It was a bit overwhelming but I was grateful for the opportunity.

During preparation for this dinner prayer where I was the honored guest, I felt the need to lend a hand and help out as much as I could. I didn't like the idea of sitting idle while others did all the hard work. My cousin Benjamin was gracious enough to hand me the knife and took a picture of me standing next to a lamb he had recently finished slaughtering for dinner. I thought a picture of me with the lamb would be a cool post on my social media.

At my uncle *Ogua's* house where I spent most of my time, my cousins were trying to box me into a corner and I wasn't going down without a fight. I needed to show and prove to them I wasn't afraid of a little hard work or getting my hands dirty. So one Saturday morning I decided to join my uncle and the boys on a trip to his farm located just outside of town near the UN Malakal site. I thought I would have no trouble keeping up with the guys and helping my uncle with the work. I thought, *how bad can it be?*

We started off pretty good walking toward the farm. Two of my cousins were carrying a petro-powered water pump. I insisted on helping to carry it as well from time to time to give the guys a break. We walked for about an hour carrying the pump and it started to get pretty heavy. I didn't want to start complaining about the distance, the heat, or the fact we did not take a water break. The guys were watching and I refused to give them any more ammunition so I kept my mouth shut.

We finally arrived at the farm and started going to work right away. Right off the bat, the work proved more difficult than I was prepared for. But still, I refused to quit because I knew the guys were expecting it and were probably thinking it was just a matter of time before the "kid coming from aboard" proved he was not up to task. I wasn't going to allow that to happen because I would never hear the end of it. I knew the jokes would follow after; it would have been brutal for the remainder of my time in Malakal.

By the grace of God I somehow managed to hold on, not faint from the heat, and proved not to be completely useless. After working all day we gathered fresh *o-dunj* also known as *kuthra* or *mulokhia* in Arabic for dinner that night. It is a spinach-like leaf sometimes called Egyptian spinach and it is my favorite dish. I was very much looking forward to enjoying it that night with *Ayodd* or *kisra* which is a thin fermented bread-like dish made from wheat.

Once we made it back from the farm, I decided to take a shower to help cool my aching body especially my feet and wait for dinner. I then joined my uncle and cousins under the bright moonlit sky and listened to him share stories about growing up in Grandpa Samuel's household and about Mom as little girl. It was strange to hear stories about my mother as a girl or about her at all from anyone else besides her.

Finally, the moment of truth arrived and dinner was served. I don't know if I will ever forget how amazing that meal was and honestly, I'm not sure if it was simply because my aunt *Nyaqua* is an amazing cook and did a wonderful job preparing the meal, or the food tasted excellent as a direct result of the kind of day I had. Either way, I enjoyed that hard-earned meal and committed to memory how difficult of a job farming really was, how much energy it exhausts and the physical toll it takes to get the job done.

CHAPTER 20

Conclusion

———

On the day of the prayer gathering at my father's house, I decided to take time to organize my thoughts on paper. I knew I had to speak a few words during the ceremony, and I wanted to make sure those words were meaningful and prepared. I was also mindful of the fact my public speaking skills were still in need of work and I did not want to embarrass myself or my family by rambling or spewing nonsense. My dad volunteered to be my translator and help communicate my words to the attendees in *Dhok Cøllø*.

The letter summarizes my thoughts and feelings about my experience up until that point. I attempted to share those thoughts and feelings with my family. When I addressed the crowd, I did not feel nervous as I normally do in front of an audience, and I did not worry about what they were thinking. My only focus was to communicate my thoughts and feelings as best as I possibly could. This was my opportunity to truly share with them who I was after all the years, and how I became the young man standing before them. I needed to share a part of my story and my unique journey from Sudan, to Egypt, to the United States and back home to my family.

THE LETTER TO MY FAMILY

Olwak Onwar Abathur
December 29, 2012

Dear Family,

First of all, I would like to thank everyone for coming out to be here today. I would like to thank my family for preparing this welcoming occasion and gathering. I would like to thank all the family friends who are here today, as well as those who could not attend.

When I left Khartoum well over twelve years ago, I never thought I would be leaving home for so long. I also never thought I would be coming back over a decade later to a split country to the Republic of South Sudan as the newest nation on the Earth. But nevertheless, I'm proud and very happy to be here.

Growing up while abroad was difficult for me. I always felt an absence in my heart—the presence of most of my family. Absent was the presence of my culture, my native tongue (*Dhok Cøllø*), and the strong spirit of the *Cøllø* community I am witnessing and feeling today. Before I left Sudan, I grew accustomed to the family-oriented lifestyle I was raised in. I was used to seeing family members on a daily basis as I have been doing over the last few weeks here in Malakal.

In the US that was not the case. I had one relative living about an hour's drive away from us with her family. We were lucky to see them once or twice a year. That posed a huge challenge for me growing up. I always wanted to be around family, but the problem was I was far away from them. That was the case until six to seven years ago when another one of my aunties and her family moved to live with us in Buffalo, New York. Before then, all I had was my immediate family—my mother and siblings.

That is, of course, why thanks and credit must be given to my mother, who could not be here with us today because she is halfway around the world. My mother is the most important person in my life. Without her guidance, love, and care, I wouldn't be here in front of you as the son, nephew, grandson to some of you older loved ones, and the young man I am today.

I wasn't always the best behaved child or the best student among other children. But over the years my mother taught me the importance and value of education, respect, family, and building good relationships with other people. She raised me the best she could for which I am very thankful. I am thankful because she struggled to do so much for me and my family, and I'm sure my father and all the family members here today are thankful as well.

Again, I would like to thank my father for opening his home to me and receiving me with open arms and a warm welcome. I would like to thank all my aunties, uncles, cousins, and other family members for helping to prepare this gathering. I would once again like to thank the family friends for being here today. Thank you all for your love and support, and for ensuring I always have a home and a family waiting for me.

Thank you,
Jenaro Olwak Onwar Abathur

Appendix

——

CHAPTER 1

"Africa's Biggest Refugee Camps." Africa Facts. Accessed March 5, 2021. https://africa-facts.org/africas-biggest-refugee-camps/.

CHAPTER 3

"South Sudan Profile – Timeline." *BBC News*, Accessed March 5, 2021. https://www.bbc.com/news/world-africa-14019202.

CHAPTER 4

"Billie Jean by Michael Jackson." Song Facts. Accessed March 5, 2021. https://www.songfacts.com/facts/michael-jackson/billie-jean.

"Daniel Camboni." Vatican. Accessed March 5, 2021. https://www.vatican.va/news_services/liturgy/saints/ns_lit_doc_20031005_comboni_en.html.

"I Will Always Love You by Whitney Houston." Song Facts. Accessed March 5, 2021. https://www.songfacts.com/facts/whitney-houston/i-will-always-love-you.

McTiernan, John, dir. *Predator*. Los Angeles, CA: Twentieth Century Studios, 1987.

Morris, Wesley. "1985: When 'Rambo' Tightened His Grip on the American Psyche." *The New York Times*. May 30, 2020. https://www.nytimes.com/2020/05/28/movies/rambo-first-blood-box-office.html.

CHAPTER 7
"1994 FIFA World Cup USA." FIFA, Accessed March 5, 2021. https://www.fifa.com/worldcup/archive/usa1994/.

"1998 FIFA World Cup FRANCE." FIFA, Accessed March 5, 2021. https://www.fifa.com/worldcup/archive/france1998/teams/team/43924/.

CHAPTER 9
Avildsen, John G., dir. *The Karate Kid*. Culver City, CA: Columbia Pictures, 1984.

CHAPTER 13
"Frequently Asked Questions." UNHCR The UN Refugee Agency USA, Accessed March 5, 2021. UNHCR - Frequently Asked Questions.

"US Annual Refugee Resettlement Ceilings and Number of Refugees Admitted, 1980-Present." MPI. Accessed March 5, 2021. https://www.migrationpolicy.org/programs/data-hub/charts/us-annual-refugee-resettlement-ceilings-and-number-refugees-admitted-united.

CHAPTER 15

"Eddy Gordo." Comic Vine. Accessed March 5, 2021. https://comicvine.gamespot.com/eddy-gordo/4005-59561/.

Goncalves-Borrega, Juan. "How Brazilian Capoeira Evolved From a Martial Art to an International Dance Craze." *Smithsonian Magazine*, September 21, 2017. https://www.smithsonianmag.com/smithsonian-institution/capoeira-occult-martial-art-international-dance-180964924/.

CHAPTER 16

"A Brief History of ROTA." Reach Out to Africa. Accessed March 5, 2021. http://reachingout2africa.com/.

CHAPTER 17

"Shufto Soccer Initiative, Inc." Shufto Soccer, Accessed March 5, 2021. https://shuftosoccer.com/.

"Taceuss. Trans-Atlantic Consortium for European Union Studies & Simulations EuroSim." Canisius. Accessed March 5, 2021. https://www3.canisius.edu/~eurosim/home.html.